Easy Living
CROCHET™

EDITED BY CAROL ALEXANDER

HOUSE of
WHITE
BIRCHES

PUBLISHERS
SINCE 1947

Easy Living Crochet™

EDITOR	Carol Alexander
ASSOCIATE EDITORS	Jessie Brinneman, Cathy Reef, Brenda Stratton
TECHNICAL EDITOR	Agnes Russell
COPY EDITORS	Conor Allen, Michelle Beck, Marla Freeman, Nicki Lehman, Beverly Richardson
PRODUCTION ASSISTANT	Marj Morgan
TECHNICAL ARTIST	Nicole Gage
PUBLISHING SERVICES MANAGER	Brenda Gallmeyer
ART DIRECTOR	Brad Snow
ASSISTANT ART DIRECTOR	Nick Pierce
GRAPHIC ARTS SUPERVISOR	Ronda Bechinski
GRAPHIC ARTIST	Pam Gregory
BOOK DESIGN	Karen Allen
COVER DESIGN	Erin Augsburger
PHOTOGRAPHY	Tammy Christian, Carl Clark, Christena Green, Matthew Owen, Nancy Sharp
PHOTOGRAPHY STYLIST	Tammy Nussbaum
CHIEF EXECUTIVE OFFICER	John Robinson
PUBLISHING DIRECTOR	David J. McKee
MARKETING DIRECTOR	Dan Fink
EDITORIAL DIRECTOR	Vivian Rothe

Printed in China
First Printing: 2005
Library of Congress Control Number: 2004113510
Hardcover ISBN: 1-59217-067-6
Softcover ISBN: 1-59217-068-4

1 2 3 4 5 6 7 8 9

Welcome!

Whether you are a beginner or seasoned crocheter, great-looking projects that are fun to make and easy to complete are always appreciated. I have heard many crocheters lament the fact that with their busy schedules today, they simply do not have a lot of spare time to devote to crochet. They want patterns that are creative and appealing, simple enough to stitch without constant frustration and don't take long, tedious periods of time to complete.

For *Easy Living Crochet*, we sought the help of many talented crochet designers to create this collection of more than 65 tantalizing, stress-busting patterns that are sure to provide many soothing hours of happy stitching. While some of the projects are large pieces, such as afghans or sweaters, many of them are small enough to easily fit in a carry-along bag when visiting family and friends or on-the-go in the car. But big or small, they are all a joy to stitch and easy to complete in whatever time you have to crochet.

You'll find simple yet stylish fashions and accessories to dress up the family, and lots of fun, useful patterns to make leisure time and travel more comfortable and enjoyable. Also included are easy home accents to punch up your decor with cozy throws, trendy pillows, dazzling table toppers and colorful rugs.

Whether you take a few hours, evenings or days, I know that you will enjoy the time spent crocheting the projects in this book. To paraphrase a well-known song lyric, "it's crochet time, and the stitching is easy."

Happy crocheting,

Carol Alexander

Contents

Crochet for Style

Crochet for Fun

Crochet for Home

Crochet for Style

Crocheted garments and accessories are the hottest additions to today's contemporary wardrobes, with ultra-cool designs that are the perfect fashion statements for expressing a winning sense of style. With the designs we have included here, you can add fun, flair and fashionable good looks to your wardrobe year-round.

Shadow Box

DESIGN BY
MARGRET WILLSON

Small recessed squares formed with long stitches create the textured, shadow box effect in this cleverly designed pullover with the look of a classic cardigan.

Intermediate •••

Size

Small [medium, large, extra-large, extra-extra-large]

Finished bust: 36 [40, 44, 48, 52] inches

Back length: 22 [22½, 23, 23½, 24] inches

Pattern is written for smallest size with changes for larger in brackets.

Materials

- Louet Sales Gems Merino Pearl fine (fingering) weight yarn (1.75 oz/185 yds/50g per hank):
  13 [14, 16, 18, 19] hanks #3 crabapple blossom
  1 [1, 1, 2, 2] hanks #6 natural
  1 hank #4 fern green
- Sizes F/5/3.75mm and G/6/4mm crochet hooks or sizes needed to obtain gauge
- Yarn needle
- ¾-inch buttons: 6

Gauge

Size G hook: 23 sts = 4 inches; 14 rows = 4 inches

Check gauge to save time.

Pattern Notes

Weave in loose ends as work progresses.

Join rounds with a slip stitch unless otherwise stated.

Back

Row 1 (RS): With crabapple blossom and size F hook, ch 111 [123, 135, 147, 159] dc in 4th ch from hook, dc in each rem ch across, change to size G hook, turn. *(109 [121, 133, 145, 157] dc)*

Row 2: Ch 2 *(counts as first hdc throughout)*, [fpdc *(see Stitch Guide)* around each of next 2 sts, dc in next st] across, ending with hdc in last st, turn.

Row 3: Ch 2, dc in each of next 2 sts, [fpdc around next st, dc in each of next 2 sts] across, ending with hdc in last st, turn.

Rows 4–51: Rep rows 2 and 3. At the end of row 51, fasten off.

Underarm shaping

Row 52: Sk next 12 [15, 15, 18, 21] sts, attach crabapple blossom in next st, ch 2, work in pattern across, leaving rem 12 [15, 15, 18, 21] sts unworked, turn.

Rows 53–81 [53–83, 53–85, 53–87, 53–89]: Work even in pattern on rem 85 [91, 103, 109, 115] sts. At the end of last rep, fasten off.

Right Front

Row 1: With crabapple blossom and size F hook, ch 51 [57, 63, 69, 75] dc in 4th ch from hook, dc in each rem ch across, change to size G hook, turn. *(49 [55, 61, 67, 73] sts)*

Rows 2–51: Work in pattern as for back. At the end of row 51, fasten off.

Underarm shaping

Row 52: Sk next 12 [15, 15, 18, 21] sts, attach crabapple blossom in next st, ch 2, work in pattern across, turn. *(37 [40, 46, 49, 52] sts)*

Rows 53–60 [53–60, 53–62, 53–62, 53–64]: Work even in pattern rows.

Neck shaping

Rows 61–80 [61–82, 63–84, 63–86, 65–88]: Maintaining pattern rows, **dc dec** *(see Stitch Guide)* in 2 sts at neck edge every row. *(17 [18, 24, 25, 28] sts)*

Row 81 [83, 85, 87, 89]: Work pattern row 3 across, fasten off.

Left Front

Rows 1–51: Rep rows 1–51 of right

front. At the end of row 51, do not fasten off.

Underarm shaping

Row 52: Work in pattern across 37 [40, 46, 49, 52] sts, turn leaving rem 12 [15, 15, 18, 21] sts unworked.

Rows 53–81 [53–83, 53–85, 53–87, 53–89]: Work as for right front.

Sleeve

Make 2.

Row 1 (RS): With size F hook and crabapple blossom, ch 54, dc in 4th ch from hook, dc in each rem ch across, change to size G hook, turn. *(52 dc)*

Rows 2–70 [2–70, 2–70, 2–70, 2–68]: Work in pattern as for back increasing 1 st at each end of row every 2 rows 0 [2, 11, 20, 28] times,

then every 3 rows 14 [22, 16, 10, 4] times, then every 4 rows 7 [0, 0, 0, 0] times. *(94 [100, 106, 112, 116] sts)*

Rows 71–77 [71–79, 71–79, 71–81, 69–81]: Work even in pattern st across rows. At the end of last rep, fasten off.

Assembly

Sew shoulder seams, fold sleeve in half, place center top of sleeve at shoulder seam, sew last row of sleeve into arm opening and side edge of rows of sleeve to underarm shaping *(side edge of rows of sleeve are sewn to the 12 [15, 15, 18, 21] sts underarm shaping)*, sew sleeve and side seams.

Edging

Rnd 1 (RS): With size F hook,

working around entire edge of piece, attach fern green with a sc in right side seam, sc in each st to lower right corner, work 93 [93, 95, 95, 97] sc up right front edge to beg of neck shaping, sc evenly around neckline, work 93 [93, 95, 95, 97] sc evenly down left front to corner, sc in each rem st around, join in beg sc, turn.

Rnd 2 (WS): Ch 1, **sc dec** *(see Stitch Guide)* in joining and next st, *sc dec in previous st and next st, rep from * around, join in beg st, fasten off, turn.

Rnd 3 (RS): Attach natural with sc, sc in each st to corner, 3 sc in corner, sc in each st to beg of neck shaping, 2 sc at beg neck shaping, sc in each st around neck edge, 2 sc at beg of left neck shaping, sc in each st to lower left corner, 3 sc in corner, sc in each rem st around, join in beg sc.

Rnds 4–9: Ch 1, sc in each sc around, working 3 sc in each lower corner and 2 sc in each neck corner, join in beg sc. At the end of rnd 9, fasten off.

Sleeve Edging

Rnd 1 (RS): With size F hook, attach fern green in sleeve seam, ch 1, sc in each st around, join in beg sc, turn.

Rnd 2 (WS): Ch 1, sc dec in joining and next st, *2 sc dec in previous st and next st, rep from * around, join in beg st, fasten off, turn.

Rnd 3 (RS): Attach natural, ch 1, sc in each st around, join in beg sc.

Rnds 4–6: Ch 1, sc in each sc around, join in beg sc. At the end of rnd 6, fasten off.

Finishing

Sew center fronts tog from beg of neck shaping to lower front corners. Sew buttons evenly sp down center front seam. ◆

Wristlet Pouf

DESIGN BY
WHITNEY CHRISTMAS

This charming little ball of fluff is actually a small, eyelash yarn wrist purse that's the perfectly chic carryall when all you need to take along are the bare essentials.

Gauge
Size N hook: 17 sts = 6¼ inches
Check gauge to save time.

Pattern Notes
Weave in loose ends as work progresses.
Join rounds with a slip stitch unless otherwise stated.

Purse
Row 1: With size M hook and 1 strand each violet and black held tog, ch 17, change to size N hook, beg in 2nd ch from hook, [insert hook in next ch, yo, draw up a lp] across *(17 lps on hook)*, yo, draw through first lp on hook, [yo, draw through 2 lps on hook] across until 1 lp rem on hook.
Rows 2–20: Sk first vertical bar, [draw up a lp under next vertical bar] across *(17 lps on hook)*, yo, draw through first lp on hook, [yo, draw through 2 lps on hook] across until 1 lp rem on hook.
Row 21: Sk first vertical bar, [insert hook into next vertical bar, yo, draw through all lps on hook] across, fasten off.
With WS facing, fold rows 1 and 21 tog and with a length of black, whipstitch side edge of rows tog on each side of purse leaving top edge of rows 1 and 21 open. Turn purse WS out and rub each seam to fluff out the eyelash yarn over the seam.

Trim
With size H hook, attach 1 strand of black at seam joining of top opening, ch 1, 2 sc in same st, *[ch 3, 2 sc in each of next 5 sts] 3 times, ch 2, 2 sc in next st **, 2 sc in next st, rep from *, ending last rep at **, join in beg sc, fasten off.
Weave black ribbon through ch-3 sps of trim, knot ends tog. Secure ribbon knot to inside of purse. ◆

Easy ••

Size
4 x 6¼ inches

Materials
- Lion Brand Fun Fur eyelash bulky (chunky) weight yarn (1¾ oz/60 yds/50g per ball):
    1 ball #191 violet
- Medium (worsted) weight yarn (3 oz/174 yds/85g per skein):
    3 skeins black
- Size H/8/5mm crochet hook or size needed to obtain gauge
- Sizes M/13/9mm and N/15/10mm afghan hooks
- Tapestry needle
- 7⁄16-inch-wide black double-faced satin ribbon: 16 inches

Copper Elegance

DESIGNS BY
ANGEL RHETT

Experienced ••••

Size

Shell: Small [medium, large, extra-large]

Shawl: 20½ x 50 inches, excluding fringe

Pattern is written for smallest size with changes for larger in brackets.

Materials

- Berroco Metallic FX medium (worsted) weight soft metallic yarn (⅞ oz/85 yds/25g per hank): 20 hanks #1005 copper/black *(A)*
- Berroco Cotton Twist medium (worsted) weight soft metallic yarn (1.75 oz/85 yds/50g per hank): 9 hanks #8373 clay *(B)*
- Size G/6/4mm crochet hook or size needed to obtain gauge
- Yarn needle
- 6–7mm copper grooved brass plated beads: 190
- Craft glue

This gorgeous beaded shawl, sparkling with lustrous copper highlights, combines with a simple coordinating shell to create an elegant evening ensemble.

Gauge

10 sc = 3 inches; 12½ sc rows = 3 inches

Check gauge to save time.

Pattern Notes

Weave in loose ends as work progresses.

Join rounds with a slip stitch unless otherwise stated.

Beads available at most craft store or at: www.abeadstore.com

Special Stitch

Long single crochet (lsc): Insert hook in sc 3 rows below next sc, yo, draw up a lp level with working row, yo, draw through both lps on hook, sk st directly behind long sc.

Shell

Back

Row 1: With B, ch 83 [87, 91, 95], sc in 2nd ch from hook, sc in each rem ch across, turn. *(82 [86, 90, 94] sc)*

Row 2: Ch 1, sc in each st across, turn.

Row 3: Rep row 2.

Row 4: Ch 1, sk first st, sc across leaving last st unworked, change to A, turn. *(80 [84, 88, 92] sc)*

Row 5: Ch 1, [sc in each of next 3 sts, lsc *(see Special Stitch)* in next st] across, change to B, turn.

Row 6: Ch 1, sk first st, sc across leaving last st unworked, turn. *(78 [82, 86, 90] sc)*

Row 7: Rep row 2.

Row 8: Rep row 6, change to A, turn. *(76 [80, 84, 88] sc)*

Row 9: Rep row 5 adjusting sts so that the lsc is worked in center sc of 3-sc group of previous lsc row.

Rows 10–12: Rep row 2. At the end of row 12, change to A, turn.

Row 13: Rep row 9.

Row 14: Rep row 6. *(74 [78, 82, 86] sc)*

Row 15: Rep row 2.

Row 16: Rep row 4. *(72 [76, 80, 84] sc)*

Row 17: Rep row 9.

Rows 18–20: Rep row 2, at the end of row 20, change to A, turn.

Row 21: Rep row 9.

Note: From this point on, maintain color pattern consisting of 1 row copper/black (A) and 3 rows clay (B) throughout unless otherwise stated.

Rows 22–53: Rep rows 18–21.

Row 54: Ch 1, 2 sc in first sc, sc in each sc across to last sc, 2 sc in last sc, turn. *(74 [78, 82, 86] sc)*

Row 55: Rep row 2.

Row 56: Rep row 54. *(76 [80, 84, 88] sc)*

Row 57: Rep row 9.

Rows 58–60: Rep row 2.

Row 61: Rep row 9.

Rows 62–64: Rep rows 54–56. *(80 [84, 88, 92] sc)*

Row 65: Rep row 9.

Rows 66–68: Rep row 2.

Row 69: Rep row 9.

Rows 70–72: Rep row 2.

Row 73: Rep row 9.

Row 74: Sl st in each of first 3 sts, ch 1, sc in each st across to last 3 sts, leaving last 3 sts unworked, turn. *(74 [78, 82, 84] sc)*

Row 75: Rep row 2.

Row 76: Sl st in first sc, ch 1, sc in each sc across to last sc, leaving last sc unworked, turn. *(72 [76, 80, 82] sc)*

Row 77: Sl st in 1 [2, 2, 2] sc, ch 1, work in pattern of row 9 across to last 1 [2, 2, 2] sc, turn. *(70 [72, 76, 78] sts)*

Row 78: Sl st in 1 [1, 2, 2] sts, ch 1, sc in each st across to last 1 [1, 2, 2] sts, turn. *(68 [70, 72, 74] sts)*

Row 79: Sl st in 0 [0, 1, 2] sts, ch 1, sc across leaving rem 0 [0, 1, 2] sts unworked, turn. *(68, [70, 70, 70] sts)*

Row 80: Rep row 2.

Row 81: Rep row 9.

Rows 82–84: Rep row 2.

Row 85: Rep row 9.

Rows 86–97: Rep rows 82–85.

Rows 98 & 99: Rep row 2.

Row 100: Ch 1, work 2 [1, 1, 1] sc in first sc, sc in each sc across to last sc, work 2 [1, 1, 1] sc in last sc, turn.

Row 101: Rep row 9.

Row 102: Ch 1, 1 [2, 2, 2] sc in first sc, sc in each st across to last st 1 [2, 2, 2] sc in last st, turn.

Rows 103 & 104: Rep row 2.

Row 105: Rep row 9.

Row 106: Rep row 2.

Row 107: Ch 1, 2 [2, 2, 2] sc in first st, sc in each st across, ending with 2 [2, 2, 2] sc in last st, turn.

Row 108: Ch 1, 1 [1, 2, 2] sc in first st, sc in each st across to last st, 1 [1, 2, 2] sc in last st, turn.

Row 109: Sl st in 1 [0, 0, 0] sts, rep row 9 across to last 1 [0, 0, 0] sts, turn.

Row 110 (sizes small & medium): Sl st in next 2 [1] st, sc across leaving 2 [1] st unworked, turn.

Row 110 (sizes large & extra-large): Ch 1, [1, 2] sc in first st, sc across to last st, [1, 2] sc in last st, turn.

Size small only

Row 111: Sl st in next st, sc in each of next 14 sts, turn.

Row 112: Sl st in first st, sc in each of next 11 sts, turn.

Row 113: Sl st in each of next 2 sts, rep row 9 across rem sts, turn.

Row 114: Sl st in first st, sc in each of next 5 sts, turn.

Row 115: Ch 1, sc in each of next 3 sts, turn.

Row 116: Sl st in each of next 2 sts, sc in next 2 sts, fasten off.

Rep rows 111–116 on opposite edge of back, maintaining pattern.

Size medium only

Row 111: Sl st in first st, sc across to last st, turn.

Row 112: Sl st in first st, sc across to last st, leave last st unworked, turn.

Row 113: Sl st in each of next 2 sts, rep row 9 across 14 sts, leave rem sts unworked, turn.

Row 114: Sl st in first st, sc in each of next 11 sts, turn.

Row 115: Sl st in first st, sc in each of next 9 sts, turn.

Row 116: Sl st in first st, sc in each of next 8 sts, turn.

Row 117: Sl st in first st, rep row 9 across next 7 sts, turn.

Row 118: Sl st in first 2 sts, sc in each of next 5 sts, turn.

Row 119: Ch 1, sc in each of first 4 sts, turn.

Row 120: Sl st in each of first 2 sts, sc in each of next 2 sts, fasten off.

Rep rows 111–120 on opposite edge of back, using care to maintain pattern.

Size large only

Row 111: Ch 1, sc in each st across, turn.

Row 112: Sl st in first st, sc in each st across to last st, leave last st unworked, turn.

Row 113: Sl st in first st, rep row 9 across to last st, leaving last st unworked, turn.

Row 114: Sl st in first st, sc across leaving last st unworked, turn.

Row 115: Sl st in each of next 2 sts, sc in each of next 14 sts, leaving rem sts unworked, turn.

Row 116: Sl st in first st, sc in each of next 11 sts, turn.

Row 117: Sl st in next st, rep row 9 across 9 sts, turn.

Row 118: Sl st in next st, sc in each of next 8 sts, turn.

Row 119: Sl st in next st, sc in each of next 7 sts, turn.

Row 120: Sl st in next 2 sts, sc in each of next 5 sts, turn, do not change to A.

Row 121: Sc in each of next 4 sts, turn.

Row 122: Sl st in each of next 2 sts, sc in each of next 2 sts, fasten off.

Rep rows 111–122 on opposite edge of back, using care to maintain pattern.

Size extra-large only

Rows 111 & 112: Ch 1, sc in each st across, turn.

Row 113: Rep row 9.

Rows 114–116: Sl st in first st, sc across leaving last st unworked, turn.

Row 117: Sl st in each of next 2 sts, rep row 9 across 14 sts, leaving rem sts unworked, turn.

Row 118: Sl st in first st, sc in each of next 11 sts, turn.

Row 119: Sl st in first st, sc in each of next 9 sts, turn.

Row 120: Sl st in first st, sc in each of next 8 sts, turn.

Row 121: Sl st in first st, rep row 9 across 7 sts, turn.

Row 122: Sl st in each of next 2 sts, sc in each of next 5 sts, turn.

Row 123: Sc in each of next 4 sts, turn.

Row 124: Sl st in each of next 2 sts, sc in each of next 2 sc, fasten off.

Rep rows 111–124 on opposite edge of back, using care to maintain pattern.

Front

Rows 1–103: Rep the same as for back.

Size small only

Row 104: Ch 1, sc in each of next 25 sts, turn.

Row 105: Rep row 9.

Row 106: Ch 1, sc in each of next 22 sts, turn.

Row 107: Sl st in each of 4 sts, sc in each of next 18 sts, turn.

Row 108: Sl st in each of next 2 sts, sc in each of next 15 sts, turn.

Row 109: Rep row 9.

Row 110: Sl st in each of next 2 sts, sc in each of next 12 sts, turn.

Row 111: Sl st in each of next 2 sts, sc in each of next 9 sts, turn.

Row 112: Sl st in first st, sc across, turn.

Row 113: Rep row 9.

Row 114: Sl st in each of next 3 sts, sc in each of next 5 sts, turn.

Row 115: Sl st in first st, sc in each of next 3 sts, turn.

Row 116: Sl st in next st, sc in each of next 2 sts, fasten off.

Rep rows 104–116 on opposite front, using care to maintain pattern.

Size medium only

Row 104: Ch 1, 2 sc in first st, sc in each st across to last st, 2 sc in last st, turn.

Row 105: Rep row 9.

Row 106: Ch 1, sc in each of next 30 sts, turn.

Row 107: Sl st in each of next 6 sts, sc in each of next 24 sts, turn.

Row 108: Ch 1, sc in each of next 21 sts, turn.

Row 109: Rep row 9.

Row 110: Sl st in each of next 2 sts, sc in each of next 15 sts, turn.

Row 111: Sl st in first st, sc across leaving last st unworked, turn.

Row 112: Sl st in each of first 2 sts, sc in each rem sc across, turn.

Row 113: Rep row 9.

Row 114: Sl st in next st, sc in each rem st across, turn.

Row 115: Sl st in next st, sc in each of next 8 sts, turn.

Row 116: Sl st in next st, sc in each of next 7 sts, turn.

Row 117: Rep row 9.

Row 118: Sl st in each of next 2 sts, sc in each rem st across, turn.

Row 119: Sl st in each of next 4 sts, sc in each rem st across, turn.

Row 120: Sl st in each of next 2 sts, sc in each of next 2 sts, fasten off.

Rep rows 104–120 on opposite front, using care to maintain pattern.

Size large only

Row 104: Ch 1, 2 sc in first st, sc in each st across to last st, 2 sc in last st, turn.

Row 105: Rep row 9.

Row 106: Rep row 2.

Row 107: Ch 1, 2 sc in first sc, sc across, ending with 2 sc in last sc, turn.

Row 108: Ch 1, sc in each of next 27 sts, turn.

Row 109: Rep row 9.

Row 110: Ch 1, 2 sc in first st, sc in next 20 sts, leaving rem sts unworked, turn.

Row 111: Sl st in first st, sc across

leaving last st unworked, turn.

Row 112: Sl st in each of next 2 sts, sc in each of next 19 sts, turn.

Row 113: Rep row 9.

Row 114: Sl st in each of next 2 sts, sc in each of next 17 sts, turn.

Row 115: Sl st in next st, sc across rem sts, turn.

Row 116: Sl st in each of next 2 sts, sc in each of next 12 sts, turn.

Row 117: Rep row 9.

Row 118: Sl st in each of next 2 sts, sc in each of next 9 sts, turn.

Row 119: Rep row 115.

Row 120: Sl st in each of next 3 sts, sc in each of next 5 sts, turn.

Row 121: Rep row 9.

Row 122: Sl st in next st, sc in each of next 2 sts, fasten off.

Rep rows 104–122 on opposite front, maintaining pattern.

Size extra-large only

Row 104: Ch 1, 2 sc in first st, sc in each st across, 2 sc in last st, turn.

Row 105: Rep row 9.

Row 106: Rep row 2.

Row 107: Ch 1, 2 sc in first sc, sc across, ending with 2 sc in last sc, turn.

Row 108: Rep row 2.

Row 109: Rep row 9.

Row 110: Rep row 107.

Row 111: Ch 1, 2 sc in first sc, sc in each of next 27 sc, leaving rem sts unworked, turn.

Row 112: Sl st in each of next 3 sts, sc in rem sc across, turn.

Row 113: Rep row 9.

Row 114: Ch 1, sc in each of next 24 sts, turn.

Row 115: Sl st in each of 3 sts, sc in each of next 21 sts, turn.

Row 116: Sl st in each of 4 sts, sc in each of next 15 sts, turn.

Row 117: Rep row 9.

Row 118: Sl st in first st, sc across rem sts, turn.

Row 119: Ch 1, sc across leaving last 2 sts unworked, turn.

Row 120: Ch 1, sc in each of next 6 sts, turn.

Row 121: Rep row 9.

Row 122: Sl st in first st, sc in each of next 4 sts, turn.

Row 123: Ch 1, sc in each of next 3 sts, turn.

Row 124: Ch 1, sc in each of next 2 sts, fasten off.

Rep rows 104–124 on opposite front, maintaining pattern.

With B, sew shoulder and side seams.

Edging

Note: Work edging around neckline, armhole openings and bottom edge of shell.

Rnd 1 (RS): Attach A at seam, ch 1, sc evenly sp around opening, join in beg sc, fasten off.

Shawl

Row 1: With A, ch 276, dc in 4th ch from hook, *sc in next ch, draw up a lp ¾ inch, sk next 3 chs, (dc, ch 1, dc) in next ch, rep from *

across to last 2 chs, sk next ch, sc in last ch, turn.

Row 2: Ch 3 *(counts as first dc)*, sk first sc, dc in next dc, *sc in next ch-1 sp, draw up a ¾-inch lp, (dc, ch 1, dc) in next sc, rep from * across to last 2 sts, sk next st, sc in last st, turn.

Rows 3–67: Rep row 2. At the end of row 67, fasten off.

Edging

Rnd 1: Attach A in any st on outer edge, ch 1, sc evenly around, working 3 sc in each corner st, join in beg sc, fasten off.

Fringe

Cut 95 strands of A each 8 inches long. Starting at top corner of shawl, attach fringe down short side of shawl, across long edge of bottom and along 2nd short side of shawl. Fold a strand in half, insert hook into edge of shawl, draw strand through at fold to form a lp on hook, draw cut ends through lp on hook, pull gently to secure.

Slide a bead onto each end of each fringe and tie a knot below the bead to hold in place.

For ease in threading yarn through bead, apply a small amount of glue to end of yarn to stiffen it. This allows the beads to slip onto the yarn more easily. ◆

Polished Rocks

DESIGN BY
HILARY MURPHY

A dainty thread choker accented with glossy, polished rocks makes an eye-catching contrast in this beautiful necklace that's the perfect finishing touch for almost any outfit.

Intermediate ●●●

Size

Neck band: ½ x 11½, excluding clasp and chain

Materials

- DMC Cebelia size 20 crochet cotton (416 yds per ball):
  20 yds #816 garnet
- Size 8/1.50mm steel crochet hook or size needed to obtain gauge
- Beading needle
- Hematite chip beads or semiprecious stone chip beads: 17
- 3-inch length of chain
- Lobster clasp
- 6mm jump ring
- Stitch markers: 2

Gauge

Rnds 1 and 2 of neck band = ½ inch; 12 dc = 1 inch
Check gauge to save time.

Pattern Note

Weave in loose ends as work progresses.

Neck Band

Rnd 1 (RS): With garnet, ch 135, dc in 4th ch from hook, dc in each of next 130 chs, 5 dc in last ch, working on opposite side of foundation ch, dc in each of next 130 chs, 3 dc in next ch, join in 3rd ch of beg ch, fasten off. *(270 dc)*
Place a st marker in 3rd dc of 5-dc group at each end of rnd 1.

Bead Loops

Note: The bead lps are worked continuously from the first bead lp through the 5th bead lp.
With beading needle, thread all beads onto garnet cotton.

First loop

With RS of neck band facing, attach garnet with sl st in 25th dc from marker, ch 20, push 3 beads up next to hook, ch 21, sk next 27 dc of rnd 1, sl st in next dc, turn, working in between neck band and bead lp, sl st in each of next 14 dc, turn.

Second loop

Ch 25, push up 3 beads next to hook, ch 26, sk next 27 dc, sl st in next dc, turn, working in between neck band and bead lp, sl st in each of next 14 dc, turn.

Third loop

Ch 30, push 5 beads up next to hook, ch 31, sk next 28 dc, sl st in next dc, turn, working in between neck band and bead lp, sl st in each of next 14 dc, turn.

Fourth loop

Ch 25, push 3 beads up next to hook, ch 26, sk next 27 dc, sl st in next dc, turn, working in between neck band and bead lp, sl st in each of next 14 dc, turn.

Fifth loop

Ch 20, push 3 beads up next to hook, ch 21, sk next 27 dc, sl st in next dc, fasten off.

Finishing

Attach the 3-inch chain length to center marked dc at either end of neck band, attach the lobster clasp and jump ring to the center marked dc at opposite end of neck band. ◆

Button-Up Cover-Up

DESIGN BY
KATHERINE ENG

Intermediate ●●●

Size
Adult

Materials
- Red Heart Super Saver medium (worsted) weight yarn (6 oz/348 yds/170g per skein:
    12 oz #4387 navy fleck
- Lion Brand Thick & Quick Chenille bulky (chunky) weight yarn (75 yds per skein):
    3 skeins #246 rainbow denim
- Size H/8/5mm crochet hook or size needed to obtain gauge
- Tapestry needle
- 1-inch blue buttons: 8
- Stitch markers: 2

An eye-catching pattern of diagonal stripes creates the appealing design in this comfortable and cozy poncho featuring plush, bulky weight chenille yarn.

Gauge
(1 sc, ch-1 sp, 1 sc) = 1 inch; first 3 rows = 1 inch
Check gauge to save time.

Pattern Notes
Weave in loose ends as work progresses.
Join rounds with a slip stitch unless otherwise stated.

Front
First half
Row 1 (RS): With navy fleck, ch 90, sc in 2nd ch from hook, *ch 1, sk 1 ch, sc in next ch, rep from * across, turn. *(45 sc; 44 ch-1 sps)*
Row 2 (WS): Ch 1, sc in first sc, [ch 1, sk next ch-1 sp, sc in next sc] across, fasten off.
Row 3 (RS): Draw up a lp of rainbow denim print in first sc, ch 1, sc in first sc, *ch 1, sk next ch-1 sp, **fpdc** *(see Stitch Guide)* over next sc around sc 1 row below, ch 1, sk next ch-1 sp, sc in next sc, rep from * across, fasten off. *(23 sc; 22 fpdc)*
Row 4 (RS): Draw up a lp of navy fleck in first sc, ch 1, sc in same sc, [ch 1, sk next ch-1 sp, sc in next st] across, turn.
Rows 5–7: Rep Row 2. At the end of Row 7, fasten off.

Row 8 (RS): Draw up a lp of rainbow denim print in first sc, ch 1, sc in same sc, *ch 3, sk each of next 3 sts *(ch-1 sp, sc and ch-1 sp)*, sc in next sc, rep from * across, fasten off. *(22 ch-3 sps)*
Row 9 (RS): Draw up a lp of navy fleck in first sc, ch 1, sc in first sc, *ch 1, sc over ch-3 sp and into sc 1 row below, ch 1, sc in next sc, rep from * across, turn.
Rows 10–12: Rep row 2. At the end of row 12, fasten off.
Row 13: Rep row 3.
Rows 14–17: Rep rows 4–7.
Row 18: Rep row 8.
Rows 19–22: Rep rows 9–12.
Second half
Row 1 (RS): With RS of row 1 of first half facing and working in opposite side of foundation ch, attach navy fleck in first ch, ch 1, sc in same ch as beg ch-1, *ch 1, sk 1 ch, sc in next ch, rep from * across, turn. *(45 sc; 44 ch-1 sps)*
Rows 2–22: Rep rows 2–22 of first half.

Border
Rnd 1 (RS): Draw up a lp of rainbow denim print in end ch of

CONTINUED ON PAGE 58 ▶

Casual Stripes

DESIGN BY
MARGRET WILLSON

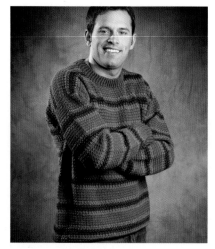

This strikingly handsome pullover is the perfect addition to a masculine, cold-weather wardrobe and is sure to be a winning choice for a special guy on your gift-giving list.

Intermediate •••

Size
Small [medium, large, extra-large, extra-extra-large]
Finished chest: 40 [44, 48, 52, 56] inches
Back length: 26 [27, 28, 29, 30] inches
Pattern is written for smallest size with changes for larger in brackets.

Materials
- CGOA Presents Frolic fine (sport) weight yarn (1.75 oz/200 yds/50g per hank):
  10 [11, 12, 13, 14] hanks #11 slate
  3 [3, 3, 4, 4] hanks each #14 basil and #16 cafe
  2 [2, 2, 2, 2] hanks #9 burgundy
- Size G/6/4mm crochet hook or size needed to obtain gauge
- Yarn needle
- Tape measure
- Stitch markers: 4

Gauge
In pattern st, 19 sts = 4 inches;
23 rows = 4 inches
Check gauge to save time.

Pattern Notes
Weave in loose ends as work progresses.
Join rounds with a slip stitch unless otherwise stated.
Rows 2 and 3 of back body establishes pattern stitch.

Back
Ribbing
Row 1 (RS): With slate, ch 97 [105, 115, 125, 133], dc in 4th ch from hook, dc in each rem ch across, turn. *(95 [103, 113, 123, 131] dc)*
Row 2: Ch 2 *(counts as first hdc throughout)*, **bpdc** *(see Stitch Guide)* around next st, [**fpdc** *(see Stitch Guide)* around next st, bpdc around next st] across, ending with hdc in last st, turn.
Row 3: Ch 2, fpdc around each fpdc and bpdc around each bpdc across, ending with hdc in last hdc, turn.
Rows 4–11: Rep row 3.
Body
Row 1 (WS): Ch 1, 2 sc in first st, sk next st, *(sc, ch 2, sc) in next st, sk next st, rep from * across, ending with 2 sc in last st, turn.
Row 2 (RS): Ch 1, sc in first sc, sk next sc, dc in sk st 1 row below, *sc in next ch-2 sp, dc in sk st 1 row below, rep from * across, ending with sc in last st, turn.
Row 3 (WS): Ch 1, 2 sc in first sc, sk next dc, *(sc, ch 3, sc) in next sc, sk next dc, rep from * across, ending with 2 sc in last sc, turn.
Rows 4 & 5: Rep rows 2 and 3 for pattern st.
Note: Beg stripe pattern, always beg new color on row 2 of pattern st.
Rows 6–132 [6–138, 6–142, 6–148, 6–154]: Rep pattern rows 2 and 3 in the following sequence: *2 rows basil, 2 rows café, 2 rows burgundy, 2 rows café, 2 rows basil, 8 [10, 10, 10, 12] rows slate, rep from * 5 more times, 2 rows basil, 2 rows café, 2 rows burgundy, 2 rows café, 2 rows basil, then work 9 [3, 7, 13, 7] rows slate, ending with pattern row 2, fasten off.

Front
Ribbing
Rows 1–11: Rep rows 1–11 of back ribbing.
Body
Rows 1–114 [1–120, 1–124, 1–130,

CONTINUED ON PAGE 59 ▶

Crimson Fire

DESIGNS BY
MARGARET HUBERT

Soft, heathery yarn in a deep, fiery red and worked in a delicately textured stitch adds subtle drama and rich detail to this stylish coat accented with a coordinating striped scarf.

Intermediate •••

Size

Ladies: Small [medium and large]
Pattern is written for smallest size with changes for larger sizes in brackets.

Materials

- Brown Sheep Lamb's Pride 1-ply medium (worsted) weight yarn (200 yds per skein):
  14 [14, 15] skeins #M181 prairie fire
  1 [1,1] skein #M145 spice
- Sizes H/8/5mm and K/10½/ 6.5mm crochet hooks or sizes needed to obtain gauge
- Tapestry needle
- 1-inch buttons: 6
- Stitch markers
- Straight pins
- 8-inch square cardboard

Gauge

Size H hook: 2 clusters = 1 inch; 6 rows = 2 inches
Size K hook: 4 clusters = 3 inches; 6 rows = 2½ inches
Check gauge to save time.

Pattern Notes

Weave in loose ends as work progresses.
Join rounds with a slip stitch unless otherwise stated.
Mark row 2 of each section as right side.

Special Stitches

Cluster (cl): (Sc, dc) in indicated st.
Decrease (dec): Ch 1, sc in first st, sc in next dc, omit the dc in this cl, continue in pattern to last cl, omit the sc, end with a dc in last cl, sc in last st.

Pattern

Row 1: (Sc, dc) in 2nd ch from hook, sk next ch, *(sc, dc) in next ch, sk next ch, rep from * across, ending with sc in last ch, turn.
Row 2: Ch 1, sc in first sc, *cl *(see Special Stitches)* in next dc, sk next sc, rep from * across, ending with sc in last sc, turn.

Coat

Back

With size H hook and prairie fire, ch 84 [88, 92] work in pattern across row. Work in row 2 of pattern until back measures 23½ [24, 24½] inches from beg. *(84 [88, 92] sts)*
To shape armholes, sl st over 4 [4, 4] sts, work across in pattern across row to last 4 [4, 4] sts, turn. *(76 [80, 84] sts)*
Continue in row 2 of pattern, **dec** *(see Special Stitches)* each side every other row 4 [4, 6] times. *(68 [72, 72] sts)*
Work in row 2 of pattern until from beg of armhole dec, armhole measures 9½ [10, 10½] inches, fasten off.

Left Front

With size H hook and prairie fire, ch 44 [46, 48] work in pattern the same as back to armhole, ending at armhole side edge. *(44 [46, 48] sts)*
To shape armhole, sl st over 4 [4, 4] sts, work in pattern across row, turn. *(40 [42, 44] sts)*
Continue in row 2 of pattern and keeping center front edge even, dec armhole edge every other row 4 [4, 6] times. *(36 [38, 38] sts)*
Work even in pattern until from

CONTINUED ON PAGE 60 ▶

Cozy Cossack

DESIGN BY
KATHLEEN
POWER JOHNSON

This cozy, Russian-style hat works up quickly and easily in deliciously warm and velvety-soft bulky chenille yarn, and makes the perfect cold-weather gift for a special guy.

Easy ••

Size

Man's: 22 inches in circumference

Materials

- Lion Brand Kool Wool bulky (chunky) weight yarn (1¾ oz/60 yds/50g per skein):
    1 skein #153 black
- Lion Brand Chenille Thick & Quick bulky (chunky) weight yarn (100 yds per skein):
    1 skein #149 gray
- Sizes J/10/6mm and K/10½/6.5mm crochet hooks or sizes needed to obtain gauge
- Yarn needle
- Stitch markers: 2

Gauge

Size J hook: 3 hdc = 1 inch; 2 hdc rows = 1 inch
Size K hook: 3 hdc = 2 inches; 4 hdc rows = 2½ inches
Check gauge to save time.

Pattern Notes

Weave in loose ends as work progresses.
Join rounds with a slip stitch unless otherwise stated.

Hat

Rnd 1 (WS): With size J hook and black, ch 19, sl st in 2nd ch from hook, sl st in each ch across to last ch, (sl st, ch 1, sl st) in last ch, working on opposite side of foundation ch, sl st in each ch across to last ch, sl st in last ch, ch 1. *(38 sts)*
Note: Place a st marker in each ch-1 sp at each end. Move st marker as work progresses.

Rnd 2: *Sl st in each st across to ch-1 sp, (sl st, ch 1, sl st) in ch-1 sp, rep from * once. *(42 sts)*
Rnds 3–7: Rep rnd 2. *(62 sts)*
Rnds 8–10: Sl st in each st around. *(62 sts)*
Rnd 11: Sc in each st around.
Rnd 12: Hdc in each st around.
Rnds 13–19: Hdc in each hdc around. At the end of rnd 19, sl st in next st, fasten off.

Brim

Rnd 1 (WS): With size K hook, attach gray, ch 1, sc around, **sc dec** *(see Stitch Guide)* 14 sts evenly sp around. *(48 sc)*
Rnds 2–4: Hdc in each st around. At the end of Rnd 4, sl st in next st, fasten off. ◆

Retro Chic

DESIGNS BY
TAMMY HILDEBRAND

Stitch this ultra-cool, charmingly retrospective bag and belt set in trendy nylon thread to add fashionable flair to a variety of outfits from casual to sophisticated.

Intermediate •••

Size

Belt: 2⅛ x 52 inches, excluding fringe
Purse: 8¾ x 9¾ inches, excluding handle and fringe

Materials

- J. & P. Coats crochet nylon 3-ply thread (150 yds per tube):
  115 yds #16 natural
  85 yds each #49 country blue and #38 celery
- Size I/9/5.5mm crochet hook or size needed to obtain gauge
- Yarn needle
- 8 x 8-inch cardboard

Gauge

6 sc = 2 inches
Check gauge to save time.

Pattern Notes

Weave in loose ends as work progresses.
Join rounds with a slip stitch unless otherwise stated.

Belt

Row 1 (RS): With celery, ch 145, sc in 2nd ch from hook, [sk next ch, 2 dc in next ch] across to last 2 chs, sk next ch, sc in last ch, fasten off. *(142 dc; 2 sc)*

Row 2 (RS): Attach country blue in first sc, ch 1, sc in same sc as beg ch-1, tr in sk ch of foundation ch, [sc in sp between next 2-dc, tr in sk ch of foundation ch] across to last sc, sc in last sc, fasten off. *(145 sts)*

Row 3 (RS): Working on opposite side of foundation ch, attach celery in first ch, ch 1, sc in same ch as beg ch-1, [sk next ch, 2 dc in next ch] across to last 2 chs, sk next ch, sc in last ch, fasten off. *(142 dc; 2 sc)*

Row 4 (RS): Rep row 2.

Border

Rnd 5 (RS): Working in ends of rows, attach natural in end of foundation ch, ch 1, sc in same ch as beg ch-1, sc in side edge of row 1, 2 sc in side edge of row 2, working in **back lps** *(see Stitch Guide)* only, sc in each st across long edge, working in ends of rows, 2 sc in first row, sc in next row, sc in opposite side of foundation ch, sc in next row, 2 sc in next row, working in back lps only, sc across long edge, working in ends of rows, 2 sc inside edge of first row, sc in next row, join in beg sc, fasten off.

Fringe

Wrap natural 3 times around cardboard, cut bottom edge of strands. Fold 3 strands in half, insert hook into end st of belt, draw strands through at fold to form a lp on the hook, draw cut ends through lp on hook, pull to secure. Work fringe in 5 sts at each end of belt.

Bag

Strip

Make 4.

Row 1 (RS): With celery, ch 48, sc in 2nd ch from hook, [sk next ch, 2 dc in next ch] across to last 2 chs, sk next ch, sc in last ch, fasten off. *(44 dc; 2 sc)*

Row 2 (RS): Rep row 2 of belt *(47 sts)*

Row 3 (RS): Rep row 3 of belt. *(44 dc; 2 sc)*

CONTINUED ON PAGE 61 ▶

Watermelon Delight Sweater

DESIGN BY
ANN SMITH

Delicious colors and a sweet design create the delectable look of this adorable sweater that's easy to make and the perfect addition to a little girl's spring wardrobe!

Intermediate ●●●

Size

Girl's 2 [4, 6]
Finished chest: 26¼ [28½, 30½] inches
Finished length: 12½ [14, 15½] inches
Pattern is written for smallest size with changes for larger sizes in brackets.

Materials

- Patons Look At Me 3-ply light (light worsted) weight yarn (1¾ oz/152 yds/50g per skein):
    4 [5, 5] skeins #6351 white
    1 skein each #6357 hot pink and #6368 kelly green
    1 yd #6364 black
- Size F/5/3.75mm crochet hook or size needed to obtain gauge
- Tapestry needle
- ⅝-inch pink buttons: 3
- ⅝-inch green buttons: 2
- Black E beads: 14
- Stitch markers

Gauge

Body pattern, 24 sts = 6 inches;
14 rows = 5 inches
Check gauge to save time.

Pattern Notes

Weave in loose ends as work progresses.
Join rounds with a slip stitch unless otherwise stated.

Special Stitch

V-stitch (V-st): (Hdc, ch 1, hdc) in indicated st.

Body Pattern

Row 1: Ch 1, hdc in first hdc, [V-st in ch-1 sp of next V-st] rep across, ending with hdc in last hdc, turn.

Back

Foundation row (RS): Beg at lower edge with white, ch 46 [50, 54], hdc in 2nd ch from hook, sk next ch, [V-st *(see Special Stitch)* in next ch, sk next ch] across, ending with hdc in last ch, turn. *(21 [23, 25] V-sts)*
Rep body pattern until from beg piece measures 6 [7, 8] inches, fasten off.

Armhole shaping

Sk first hdc and next V-st, attach white with a sl st in ch-1 sp of next

V-st, hdc in same ch-1 sp, work 17 [19, 21] V-sts across, hdc in next ch-1 sp of next V-st, turn.
Work even in row 1 of body pattern until piece from beg measures 11 [12½, 14] inches, fasten off.

Left Front

Foundation row (RS): Beg at lower edge with white, ch 24 [26, 28], hdc in 2nd ch from hook, sk next ch, [V-st in next ch, sk next ch] across, ending with hdc in last ch, turn. *(10 [11, 12] V-sts)*
Rep body pattern until from beg front measures 6 [7, 8] inches, ending last rep at neck edge.

Armhole shaping

Work in body pattern across 8 [9, 10] V-sts, hdc in next ch-1 sp, turn.
Work in body pattern until from beg front measures 8 [9½ 11] inches, ending last rep at armhole edge.

Neck shaping

Row 1: Work in body pattern across 6 [7, 8] V-sts, hdc in ch-1 sp of next V-st, turn.
Row 2: Ch 1, sc in hdc, hdc in ch-1 sp of next V-st, V-st in each of next 5 [6, 7] V-sts, hdc in last hdc, turn.
Row 3: Ch 1, hdc in hdc, V-st in each of next 5 [6, 7] V-sts, hdc in last hdc, turn.

Row 4: Ch 1, sc in hdc, hdc in next ch-1 sp of next V-st, V-st in next 4 [5, 6] V-sts, hdc in last hdc, turn.
Row 5: Ch 1, hdc in hdc, V-st in each of next 4 [5, 6] V-sts, hdc in last hdc, turn.
Row 6: Ch 1, sc in hdc, hdc in ch-1 sp of next V-st, V-st in next 3 [4, 5] V-sts, hdc in last hdc, turn.
Row 7: Ch 1, hdc in hdc, V-st in each of next 3 [4, 5] V-sts, hdc in last hdc, turn.
Rep row 7 until front measures the same length as back, fasten off.

Right Front
Rep the same as left front, reversing armhole and neck shaping.

Sleeve
Make 2.
Foundation row: Beg at lower edge, with white, ch 28 [32, 36], hdc in 2nd ch from hook, sk next ch, [V-st in next ch, sk next ch] across, turn. *(12 [14, 16] V-sts)*
Row 1: Ch 1, hdc in first hdc, (hdc, V-st) in next ch-1 sp, V-st in next 10 [12, 13] V-sts, (V-st, hdc) in next V-st, hdc in last hdc, turn.
Row 2: Ch 1, hdc in first hdc, V-st in next hdc, V-st in each V-st across to last 2 hdc, V-st in next hdc, hdc in last hdc, turn. *(14 [16, 18] V-sts)*
Row 3: Ch 1, hdc in hdc, V-st in each V-st across, hdc in last hdc, turn.
Row 4: Rep row 3.
Row 5: Ch 1, hdc in first hdc, (hdc, V-st) in next V-st, V-st in each of next 12 [14, 16] V-sts, (V-st, hdc) in next V-st, hdc in last hdc, turn.
Row 6: Ch 1, hdc in first hdc, V-st in next hdc, V-st in each V-st across to last 2 hdc, V-st in next hdc, hdc in last hdc, turn. *(16 [18, 20] V-sts)*
Rep row 3 until from beg sleeve measures 9½ [11, 12½] inches, fasten off.

Assembly
Sew shoulder seams. Place a st marker at side edge of sleeve, 1 inch from top. Set in sleeve sewing edges of armholes to rows above sleeve marker forming square armholes. Sew sleeve and side seam.

Sleeve Trim
Rnd 1 (RS): Attach white in sleeve seam, ch 1, 20 [22, 24] sc evenly sp around, join in beg sc, fasten off.
Rnd 2 (RS): Attach kelly green, ch 1, hdc in each sc around, join in beg hdc, fasten off.
Rnd 3 (RS): Attach white, ch 1, sc in each hdc around, join in beg sc, fasten off.
Rnd 4 (RS): Attach hot pink, ch 1, sc in each st around, join in beg sc, turn.
Rnd 5 (WS): Sl st in each sc around, turn.
Rnd 6 (RS): Working over last rnd and between the hot pink sc sts, [ch 1, sl st] between sts around, fasten off.

Body Band
Rnd 1 (RS): Attach white with sl st at center back of next, ch 1, work 15 sc evenly sp to shoulder seam, 21 sc evenly sp along front neck edge, 3 sc in corner, 34 [40, 46] sc evenly sp to lower edge, 3 sc in corner, sc in opposite side of foundation ch around bottom edge of sweater, 3 sc in corner, 34 [40, 46] sc evenly sp to neck edge, 3 sc in corner, 21 sc evenly sp along front neck edge, 15 sc across back neck, join in beg sc, fasten off.
Rnd 2 (RS): Attach kelly green in sc near side seam of lower edge, ch 1, hdc in each sc around, working 3 hdc in each of 4 corners and **hdc dec** *(see Stitch Guide)* st at each shoulder, join in beg hdc, fasten off.
Rnd 3 (RS): Attach white with sl st in joining, ch 1, sc in each hdc around, working 3 sc in each 4 corners and **sc dec** *(see Stitch Guide)* at each shoulder, for right front buttonholes work 3 sc in corner, sc in each of next 8 [10, 12] sts, ch 2, *ch 2, sk 2 hdc**, sc in each of next 5 [6, 7] hdc, rep from

* 4 times, ending last rep at **, 3 sc in corner st, rep in sc around, join in beg sc, fasten off.
Rnd 4 (RS): Attach hot pink with sl st in joining, ch 1, sc in each sc around, 2 sc over each ch-2 sp of each buttonhole, 3 sc in each corner and sc dec *(see Stitch Guide)* at shoulders, join in beg sc, turn.
Rnd 5 (WS): Sl st in each sc around, turn.
Rnd 6 (RS): Working over last rnd and between the hot pink sc sts, [{sl st in next st, ch 1} 6 times, sk 1 st] around, join, fasten off.

Collar
Row 1 (RS): Attach white with a sl st at right neck in rnd 1 of body band, work 73 sl sts around neckline, fasten off.
Row 2 (RS): Attach hot pink with sl st in first sl st, ch 1, sc in same st as sl st, [ch 1, sk 1 st, (hdc, 3 dc, hdc) in next st, ch 1, sk next st, sc in next st] across neckline, fasten off.
Row 3 (RS): Attach white with sl st in first sc of previous row, ch 1, sc in same sc as beg ch-1, sc in next ch-1 sp, [sc in next hdc, sc in each of next 3 dc, sc in next hdc, sc in ch-1 sp, sk next sc, sc in next ch-1 sp] across, ending with sc in last sc, fasten off.
Row 4 (RS): Attach kelly green with sl st in side edge of collar, ch 1, work 2 sc across side edge, sc in each of next 4 sc, *3 sc in next sc, sc in each of next 2 sc **, sc dec in next 2 sc, sc in each of next 2 sc, rep from * across, ending last rep at **, sc in each of next 2 sc, 2 sc along side edge of collar, turn.
Row 5 (WS): Ch 1, sl st in each of next 14 sc, [sk 1 sc, sl st in each of next 7 sc] across, ending with sl st in last 3 sc, turn.
Row 6 (RS): Ch 1, (sl st, ch 1) over last sl st row and into sp between sts of row 4 for 9 times, *sk 1 sp, in established pattern [sl st ch 1] 7 times, rep from * across, ending last

sc, sc in each sc across to last 2 sc, sk next sc, sc in last sc, turn. *(13 sc)*

Rows 8–10: Rep row 7. At the end of row 10, fasten off. *(7 sc)*

Rnd 11: Attach hot pink in opposite side of foundation ch, ch 1, sc in same ch as beg ch-1, sc in each of next 13 chs, 3 sc in last ch, sc evenly sp around pocket, ending with 2 sc in same sc as beg sc, join in beg sc, fasten off.

Row 12 (RS): Attach white in center sc of 3-sc corner, ch 1, sc in same sc as beg ch-1, sc in each sc around, ending with last sc in center sc of 3-sc group, fasten off.

Row 13 (RS): Attach kelly green in first sc of previous row, ch 1, hdc in same sc, hdc in each of next 5 sc, 2 hdc in each sc to last 6 sc, hdc in each of next 6 sc, turn.

Row 14: Sl st in each st across, turn.

Row 15: Ch 1, [(sl st, ch 1) over last sl st row and into sp between sts of row 13] across, fasten off.

Finishing

Using photo as a guide, with a length of hot pink yarn, sew 7 beads to top edge of each pocket. With kelly green, sew a pocket to each front at a slight angle. With a length of black yarn, alternating button colors, sew buttons to left front opposite buttonholes with a French knot as follows: insert needle from back to front, through hole of button, wrap yarn around needle 3 times, insert needle through rem hole of button to back of front, pull tightly, knot to secure. Rep French knot attachment with each rem button. ◆

rep, [sl st, ch 1] 10 times, fasten off.

Pocket

Make 2.

Row 1: With hot pink, ch 16, sc in 2nd ch from hook, sc in each rem ch across, turn. *(15 sc)*

Rows 2–6: Ch 1, sc in each sc across, turn.

Row 7: Ch 1, sc in first sc, sk next

Sailing Away Sweater

DESIGN BY
ANN SMITH

Sailing, sailing over the ocean blue … perfectly describes the delightful design in this cute and colorful cardigan that any little boy would love to wear!

Intermediate ● ● ●

Size

Child's: 2 [4, 6]
Finished chest: 27 [29, 31] inches
Finished length: 12½ [14, 15½] inches
Pattern is written for smallest size with changes for larger sizes in brackets.

Materials

- Patons Look At Me light (light worsted) weight yarn (1¾ oz/152 yds/50g per skein):
    4 [5, 6] skeins #6367 bright blue
    1 oz each #6366 sunny yellow,
    #6351 white and
    #6365 racy red
- Size F/5/3.75mm crochet hook or size needed to obtain gauge
- Tapestry needle
- ⅝-inch anchor buttons: 5
- Yarn bobbins
- Stitch markers

Gauge

16 sts = 4 inches; 18 rows = 4 inches
Check gauge to save time.

Pattern Notes

Weave in loose ends as work progresses.

Join rounds with a slip stitch unless otherwise stated.

The sailboats are worked in single crochet following graph, reading from right to left on right side rows and left to right on wrong side rows. The circles on graph are treble stitches that are worked on wrong side row of the sweater.

Yellow waves are crocheted on sweater after the pieces are joined.

To change yarn color, with 2 loops of working color on hook, drop yarn to wrong side, pick up next color, yarn over, draw through remaining 2 loops on hook.

Use yarn bobbins for each separate color section to keep yarns from tangling.

Special Stitch

Front post half double crochet (fphdc): Yo hook, insert hook front to back and to front again, yo, draw up a lp, yo, draw through all 3 lps on hook.

Body Pattern

Row 1 (RS): Ch 1, sc in each st across, turn.

Row 2: Ch 1, sc in first sc, [tr in next sc, sc in each of next 3 sc] across, ending with tr in next sc, sc in last sc, turn.

Rows 3–5: Rep row 1.

Row 6: Ch 1, sc in each of first 3 sc, [tr in next sc, sc in each of next 3 sc] across, ending with tr in next sc, sc in each of next 3 sc, turn.

Rows 7–9: Rep row 1.

Rep rows 2–9 for body pattern.

Back

Foundation row (RS): Beg at lower edge with bright blue, ch 52 [56, 60], sc in 2nd ch from hook, sc in each rem ch across, turn. *(51 [55, 59] sc)*

Rep row 1 of body pattern 3 times. Beg body pattern with row 1, then rep rows 2–9 for pattern until back measures from beg 11½ [13, 14½] inches, fasten off.

Right Front

Foundation row (RS): Beg at lower edge, with bright blue, ch 25 [27, 29], sc in 2nd ch from hook, sc in each rem ch across, turn. *(24 [26, 28] sc)*

Rep row 1 of body pattern 3 times. Beg right front graph with row 5,

which is a RS row. Work as graph indicates until front measures from beg 7½ inches, ending on a WS row. [**Sc dec** (*see Stitch Guide*) at neck edge every row] 3 times. *(21 [23, 25] sts)* [Sc dec in next 2 sts at neck edge every other row] 5 times. *(16 [18, 20] sts)* When graph is completed, continue to sc in each st until front measures the same as back, fasten off.

Left Front

Work as for right front following left front graph and reversing neck shaping.
Sew fronts to back at shoulders. From shoulder seam, place a marker 6 inches down on each front and back armhole edge.

Sleeve

Make 2.
Foundation row: With RS facing, attach bright blue at marker, ch 1, work 47 [51, 55] sc evenly sp between markers.
Row 1 (WS): Ch 1, sc in next 4 sts, [tr in next st, sc in each of next 3 sts] across, ending with tr in next st, sc in each of next 4 sts, turn.
Row 2: Ch 1, sc dec in next 2 sts, sc in each st across to last 2 sts, sc dec in next 2 sts, turn. *(45 [49, 53] sts)*
Row 3: Ch 1, sc in each st across, turn.
Row 4: Rep row 2. *(43 [47, 51] sts)*
Row 5: Ch 1, sc in first st, [tr in next st, sc in each of next 3 sts] across, ending with tr in next sc, sc in last sc, turn.
Rep rows 2–5 until 23 sts rem. Adjust beg and ending of row 5 as work progresses so that the tr of working row ends up centered between tr of previous tr row. Work even in pattern until sleeve measures from beg 6½ [7½, 9] inches, ending with row 5 on WS.
Cuff
Rnd 1 (RS): Ch 1, sc in each st

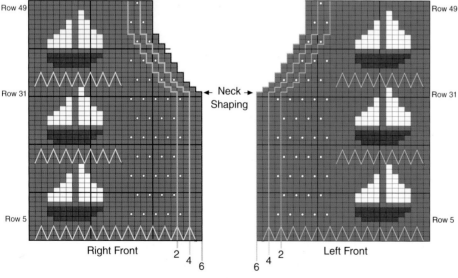

Row 49   Row 31   Row 5

← Neck → Shaping

Right Front   2   4   6

6   4   2   Left Front

Row 49   Row 31   Row 5

COLOR & STITCH KEY
◼ Blue
◼ Red
☐ White
◦ Tr Bobble
⋀ Yellow waves
× Start point for waves

CONTINUED ON PAGE 61 ▶

Red Hats Rule!

DESIGN BY
MARY LAYFIELD

Make a fun fashion statement with this easy, stylish bag stitched in size 3 cotton thread and adorned with a trio of whimsical, purple-trimmed red hats!

Gauge
Size 7 hook: 9 dc = 1 inch
Size E hook: 3 sc = ½ inch;
12 sts = 2 inches
Check gauge to save time.

Pattern Notes
Weave in loose ends as work progresses.
Join rounds with a slip stitch unless otherwise stated.

Purse
Row 1 (WS): With size E hook and new ecru, ch 78, sc in 2nd ch from hook, sc in each rem ch across, turn. *(77 sc)*
Row 2: Ch 3 *(counts as first dc throughout)*, [sk next 2 sts, tr in next st, reaching over and working behind tr, dc in first sk sc, dc in next sk sc, dc in next sc beyond previous tr] across, turn. *(19 tr; 58 dc)*
Row 3: Ch 1, sc in each st across, turn. *(77 sc)*
Rows 4–79: Rep rows 2 and 3. At the end of row 79, fasten off.

Purse Lining
Using purse as a pattern, cut fabric ½-inch larger. Leaving top of lining open, sew purse sides tog. To shape bottom, at center bottom, fold sewn corner under in the shape of the head of an arrow with the point pointing toward opposite edge of bag, tack in place. This will make a flat bottom to the lining. Rep fold on opposite edge of lining. Set lining aside.

Handle Strap
Make 10.
Row 1: With size E hook and new ecru, ch 6, sc in 2nd ch from hook, sc in each rem ch across, turn. *(5 sc)*
Rows 2–11: Ch 1, sc in each sc across, turn.
Row 12: Wrap strap around handle indent, holding row 11 to opposite side of foundation ch and working through both thicknesses, ch 1, work 5 sc across, fasten off.
Rep until 5 straps are attached to each handle.
Row 13: With RS of purse facing, working in sts of row 79, attach new ecru in first st, ch 1, sc in same st, sc in each of next 19 sts, holding handle at front and [working through both thicknesses of handle strap *(sc sts of Row 12)* and purse, sc in each of next 5 sts, working on purse sts only, sc in each of next 3 sts] 5 times, working on purse sts only, sc in each of next 20 sts, fasten off.

Easy ••

Size
10 x 11 inches, excluding handles

Materials
- J. & P. Coats Speed-Cro-Sheen size 3 crochet cotton (100 yds per ball):
    5 balls #61 new ecru
- South Maid crochet cotton size 10 (350 yds per ball):
    175 yds #494 victory red
    100 yds #458 purple
- Size 7/1.65mm steel crochet hook or size needed to obtain gauge
- Size E/4/3.5mm crochet hook or size needed to obtain gauge
- Tapestry needle
- Sewing needle
- Thread
- Darice amber purse handles #1972-15
- 14½ x 25 inches red lining fabric
- Straight pins

Rep row 13 on opposite side of foundation ch.

Purse Joining

With RS facing, holding edges tog, with size E hook, attach new ecru in side top edge, ch 1, working through both thicknesses down side edge, sc evenly sp to bottom edge, leaving a length of cotton, fasten off. Rep joining on opposite edge, then work fold at bottom in same manner as lining to create a bottom edge to purse. Turn purse right side out.

Insert lining into purse, turn top edge under and pin in place. Sew top edge of lining just below row 13 of attaching straps to purse.

First Hat

Note: Hat is located on purse at top right with 2 flowers.
Row 1: With size E hook and 2 strands of victory red held tog, ch 4, sc in 2nd ch from hook, sc in each of next 2 chs, turn. *(3 sc)*
Row 2: Ch 1, 2 sc in each sc across, turn. *(6 sc)*

Row 3: Ch 2 *(counts as first hdc throughout)*, hdc in same st as beg ch-2, hdc in each st across to last st, 2 hdc in last st, turn. *(8 hdc)*
Rows 4 & 5: Rep row 3. *(12 hdc)*
Row 6: Ch 2, hdc in each hdc across, turn.
Row 7: Rep row 3, fasten off victory red, turn. *(14 hdc)*
Row 8: Attach 2 strands of purple, rep Row 3. *(16 hdc)*
Row 9: Ch 1, sc in each st across, fasten off, turn.

Row 10: Attach 2 strands of victory red, ch 2, 2 hdc in next st, [hdc in next st, 2 hdc in next st] across, turn. *(24 hdc)*

Row 11: Ch 2, hdc in next st, [2 hdc in next st, hdc in each of next 3 sts] 5 times, 2 hdc in next st, hdc in last st, turn. *(30 hdc)*

Row 12: Ch 2, 2 hdc in next st, [hdc in each of next 3 sts, 2 hdc in next st] 7 times, fasten off. *(38 hdc)*

Flower

Make 2.

Row 1: With size 7 hook and 1 strand of purple, ch 31, dc in 4th ch from hook, dc in each of next 2 chs, ch 2, sc in next ch, *ch 2, dc in each of next 3 chs, ch 2, sc in next ch, rep from * across, leaving an 18-inch length of cotton, fasten off. *(7 petals)*

Thread cotton onto tapestry needle, starting at the end that has the rem length, start rolling flower, tack bottom edge tog as the flower is rolled, continue to the end, tack flower to purple section of hat. Using photo as a guide, sew hat to purse.

Second Hat

Note: Hat is located on purse at top left with 1 flower.

Row 1: With size E hook and 2 strands of victory red, ch 14, sc in 2nd ch from hook, sc in each rem ch across, turn. *(13 sc)*

Row 2: Ch 2 *(counts as first hdc throughout)*, hdc in same st as beg ch-2, hdc in each st across to last st, 2 hdc in last st, turn. *(15 hdc)*

Row 3: Rep row 2. *(17 hdc)*

Row 4: Ch 2, hdc in each st across, turn.

Row 5: Ch 1, sk first hdc, sc in 2nd hdc, hdc in each of next 13 hdc, sc in next hdc, fasten off leaving rem st unworked. *(15 sts)*

Row 6: Working in opposite side of foundation ch, attach 2 strands of purple in first ch, ch 1, sc in same ch, sc in each of next 12 chs, turn. *(13 sc)*

Row 7: Ch 1, sc in each sc across, fasten off, turn.

Row 8: With 2 strands of victory red, ch 7, working across sc of Row 7, sc in each of next 13 sc, turn.

Row 9: Ch 8, sc in 2nd ch from hook, sc in next ch, hdc in each of next 5 chs, hdc in next sc, [2 dc in next sc, dc in next sc] 3 times, [2 tr in next sc, tr in next sc] 3 times, 2 dc in next ch, dc in each of next 2 chs, hdc in each of next 2 chs, sc in each of next 2 chs, turn.

Row 10: Ch 1, sc in first st, [ch 2, sc in next st] 14 times, [ch 1, sc in next st] 13 times, ch 1, [sk next st, sc in next st] 3 times, fasten off.

Rose

Row 1: With steel size 7 hook and 1 strand of purple, ch 47, dc in 4th ch from hook, dc in each rem ch across, turn. *(45 dc)*

Row 2: Ch 3, dc in each of next 3 dc, ch 2, sc in next dc, *ch 2, dc in each of next 3 dc, ch 2, sc in next dc, rep from * across, leaving a length of crochet cotton, fasten off. Thread crochet cotton onto tapestry needle, starting at the end that has the rem length, start rolling flower, tack bottom edge tog as the flower is rolled, continue to end, tack to secure end.

Leaf

Make 2.

Row 1: With size 7 hook and 1 strand of purple, ch 8, sc in 2nd ch from hook, hdc in next ch, dc in each of next 2 chs, hdc in next ch, sc in next ch, ch 10, sc in 2nd ch from hook, hdc in next ch, dc in each of next 5 chs, hdc in next ch, sc in next ch, ch 8, sc in 2nd ch from hook, hdc in next ch, dc in each of next 2 chs, hdc in next ch, sc in next ch, sl st in last ch, ch 5, fasten off.

Tack the ch-5 on underneath side of rose and place rose on hat with leaves spreading to each side. Using photo as a guide, turn wide portion of rim underneath back of hat and with victory red crochet cotton tack to hat, then let front portion of rim turn upward, tack in place, tack hat to purse.

Third Hat

Note: Hat is at lower center.

Row 1: With size E hook and 2 strands of victory red, ch 5, sc in 2nd ch from hook, sc in each rem ch across, turn. *(4 sc)*

Row 2: Ch 2 *(counts as first hdc throughout)*, hdc in same st as beg ch-2, 2 hdc in each st across, turn. *(8 hdc)*

Row 3: Ch 2, hdc in same st as beg ch-2, hdc in each st across to last st, 2 hdc in last st, turn. *(10 hdc)*

Rows 4 & 5: Ch 1, sc in each st across, turn.

Rnd 6: Working in **front lps** *(see Stitch Guide)* of sc sts of row 5, sc in each of next 10 sts, working across rem back lps of row 5, sc in each of next 10 sts, sl st to join in beg sc. *(20 sc)*

Rnd 7: Ch 3 *(counts as first dc throughout)*, dc in same st as beg ch-3, 2 dc in each sc around, join in 3rd ch of beg ch-3. *(40 dc)*

Rnd 8: Ch 3, 2 dc in next dc, [dc in next dc, 2 dc in next dc] around, join in 3rd ch of beg ch-3. *(60 dc)*

Rnd 9: Ch 3, dc in each of next 2 dc, 2 dc in next dc, [dc in each of next 3 dc, 2 dc in next dc] around, join in 3rd ch of beg ch-3, fasten off. *(75 dc)*

Rnd 10: With size 7 hook, attach 1 strand of purple in any dc of rnd 9, ch 1, sc in same st as beg ch-1, ch 1, [sc in next dc, ch 1] around, join in beg sc, fasten off.

Rose

Rep rose as for second hat.

Leaf

Make 2.

Rep leaf as for second hat. Using photo as a guide, sew rose and leaf groups to purple section of hat. Sew hat centered below to hats above. ◆

Flowering Vines

DESIGNS BY
GWEN BLAKLEY KINSLER

Use small amounts of colorful, trendy yarns to enhance a plain denim shirt with glitzy flowers that spill over the neck and shoulders, making it a one-of-a-kind fashion sensation.

Easy ••

Size
Petal flowers: 2½–3 inches in diameter
Popcorn buds: 1 inch in diameter
Leaf: 2–3 inches

Materials
- Variety of novelty yarns as desired:
  Filature di Crosa No Smoking glitter yarn (83 yds/25g per skein):
      1 skein #135 red
- DMC Pearl size 8 cotton:
      50g ball each green and light green
- Novena by Skacel
  Firenza by Schewe
  Hobby Kids
- Size G/6/4mm crochet hook or size needed to obtain gauge
- Tapestry needle
- Sewing needle
- Thread
- Straight pins
- Long sleeve denim shirt

Gauge
4 sts = 1 inch
Check gauge to save time.

Pattern Notes
Weave in loose ends as work progresses.
Join rounds with a slip stitch unless otherwise stated.

Special Stitches
Popcorn (pc): 5 dc in indicated st, draw up a lp, remove hook, insert hook in first dc of 5-dc group, pick up dropped lp and draw through st on hook, ch 1 to lock.

Backstitch: Embroider short even sts used to attach crochet motifs to fabric. It requires a specific stitching sequence: take the first st backward, bring up needle 2 st lengths in direction you'll be traveling, then insert needle in the same hole where the previous st began.

Flower
Make 2 each of no smoking, novena and hobby kids.
Rnd 1 (RS): Ch 4, sl st to join to form a ring, ch 1, 8 sc in ring, join in beg sc. *(8 sc)*
Rnd 2: Working in **back lps** (*see Stitch Guide*) only, ch 1, sc in same st as beg ch-1, ch 3, sk next st, [sc in next st, ch 3, sk next st] 3 times, join in beg sc. *(4 ch-3 lps)*
Rnd 3: Sl st into ch-3 lp, ch 1, (sc, hdc, 3 dc, hdc, sc) in each ch-3 sp around, join in beg sc. *(4 petals)*
Rnd 4: Sl st behind petal and into next sk sc of rnd 1, ch 1, sc in same sc, ch 3, [sc in next sk sc of rnd 1, ch 3] 3 times, join in beg sc. *(4 ch-3 lps)*
Rnd 5: Sl st into ch-3 sp, ch 1, (sc, hdc, 5 dc, hdc, sc) in each ch-3 sp around, join in beg sc, fasten off. *(4 petals)*

Leaf
Make 7 with pearl cotton and 3 with pompom.
Row 1: Ch 15, sc in 2nd ch from hook, hdc in next ch, dc in each of next 3 chs, tr in each of next 4 chs, dc in each of next 3 chs, hdc in next ch, 3 sc in last ch, working on opposite side of foundation ch, sc in next ch, hdc in next ch, dc in each of next 3 chs, tr in each of next 4 chs, dc in each of next 3 chs, hdc in next ch, sc in next ch, sl st in next st, fasten off.

Flower Bud
Make 2 each with no smoking and hobby kids.

CONTINUED ON PAGE 62 ▶

Sophisticated Shells Cardigan

DESIGN BY
MELISSA LEAPMAN

A chic combination of trendy yarn and jazzy colors gives new flair to a classic shell design in this simple yet sophisticated cardigan with a winning look that's fresh and fashionable.

Intermediate •••

Size

Bust (buttoned): 36½ [40¼, 44¼, 48¼, 52¼] inches

Pattern is written for smaller size with changes for larger sizes in brackets.

Materials

- Patons Katrina medium (worsted) weight yarn (3½ oz/163 yds/100g per skein):
  5 [6, 7, 8] skeins #10315 iris (A)
  4 [5, 5, 6] skeins #10742 lagoon (B)
  5 [5, 6, 6] skeins #10712 limon (C)
- Yarn needle
- Size H/8/5mm crochet hook or size needed to obtain gauge
- ¾-inch buttons: 6
- Stitch markers

Gauge

In shell pattern, 16 sts = 4 inches; 11 rows = 4 inches

Check gauge to save time.

Pattern Notes

Weave in loose ends as work progresses.

Join rounds with a slip stitch unless otherwise stated.

Each single crochet, double crochet, and beginning ch-3 counts as first stitch.

Color sequence of one row each is [A, B, C] rep for pattern.

Shell Pattern

Foundation row (RS): Sc in 2nd ch from hook, [sk next ch, 3 dc in next ch, sk next ch, sc in next ch] across, change color, turn.

Row 1 (WS): Ch 3, dc into first st, [sk next dc, sc in next dc, sk next dc, 3 dc in next sc] across, ending with sk next dc, sc in next dc, sk next dc, 2 dc in last sc, change color, turn.

Row 2: Ch 1, sc in first dc, [sk next dc, 3 dc in next sc, sk next dc, sc in next dc] across, ending with sk next dc, 3 dc in next sc, sk next dc, sc in 3rd ch of beg ch-3, change color turn.

Rep rows 1 and 2 for pattern.

Back

With A, ch 74 [82, 90, 98, 106], beg shell pattern in color sequence and work even on 73 [81, 89, 97, 105] sts until piece measures approximately 17½ inches from beg, ending after a row 2 of pattern, fasten off.

Armhole shaping

With WS facing, sk first 8 [8, 8, 12, 12] sts, attach next color with a sl st to next st, ch 3, complete row same as row 1 of shell pattern until 8 [8, 8, 12, 12] sts rem in row, change color, turn, leaving rem sts unworked.

Ch 1, continue even on 57 [65, 73, 73, 81] sts until piece measures approximately 25 [25, 26, 26, 26] inches from beg, ending with a row 1 of shell pattern, change color, turn.

First neck shaping

With RS facing, ch 1, sc in first dc, [sk next dc, 3 dc in next sc, sk next dc, sc in next dc] 3 [4, 5, 5, 6] times, sk next dc, 2 dc in next sc, change color, turn.

Ch 1, continue even on 15 [19, 23, 23, 27] sts until piece measures approximately 26 [26, 27, 27, 27] inches from beg, fasten off.

Second neck shaping

With RS facing, sk the center 27 sts for neckline opening, attach yarn with sl st into next st, ch 3, complete same as first side.

Left Front

With A, ch 34 [38, 42, 46, 50], beg

shell pattern in color sequence, work even on 33 [37, 41, 45, 49] sts until piece measures approximately 17½ inches from beg, ending with a row 2 pattern row, fasten off.

Armhole shaping

With WS facing, sk first 8 [9, 8, 12, 12] sts, attach next color with a sl st in next st, ch 3, complete row same as row 1 of shell pattern. Continue even on 25 [29, 33, 33, 37] sts until piece measures approximately 18½ [18½, 19½, 19½, 19½] inches from beg, ending after a RS row, change color, turn.

Neck shaping

Row 1: With WS facing, ch 2, sk first sc and dc, [sc in next dc, sk next dc, 3 dc in next sc, sk next dc] across, ending row with sc in next dc, sk next dc, 2 dc in last sc, change color, turn.

Row 2: Ch 1, [sc in dc, sk next dc, 3 dc in next sc, sk next dc] across, ending row with sc in next dc, sk next dc, 2 dc in next sc, change color, turn.

Row 3: Ch 3, [sc in next dc, sk next dc, 3 dc in next sc, sk next dc] across, ending row with sc in dc, sk next dc, 2 dc in last sc, change color, turn.

Row 4: Ch 1, [sc in next dc, sk next dc, 3 dc in next sc, sk next dc] across, ending row with sc in next dc, sk next dc, hdc in last sc, change color, turn.

Row 5: Ch 3, sk hdc, dc in next sc, sk next dc, [sc in next dc, sk next dc, 3 dc in next sc, sk next dc] across, ending row with sc in next dc, sk next dc, 2 dc in last sc, change color, turn.

Row 6: Ch 1, [sc in next dc, sk next dc, 3 dc in next sc, sk next dc] across, ending row with sc in next dc, sk next dc, 2 dc in next sc, hdc in next dc, change color, turn.

Row 7: Ch 3, sk hdc, [sc in next dc, sk next dc, 3 dc in next sc, sk next dc] across, ending row with sc in next dc, sk next dc, 2 dc in next sc, change color, turn.

Row 8: Ch 1, [sc in next dc, sk next dc, 3 dc in next sc, sk next dc] across, ending with sc in next dc, sk next dc, dc and hdc in last sc, change color, turn.

Row 9: Ch 1, sc in hdc, sk dc, [3 dc in next sc, sk next dc, sc in next dc, sk next dc] across, ending row with 2 dc in last sc, change color, turn.

Row 10: Ch 1, [sc in next dc, sk next dc, 3 dc in next sc, sk next dc] across, ending row with sc in dc, sk next dc, dc and hdc in last sc, change color, turn.

Row 11: Ch 1, sc into hdc, sk next dc, 2 dc in next sc, sk next dc, [sc in next dc, sk next dc, 3 dc in next sc, sk next dc] across, ending row with sc in dc, sk next dc, 2 dc in last sc, change color, turn.

Row 12: Ch 1, [sc in next dc, sk next dc, 3 dc in next sc, sk next dc]

across, ending row with sc in dc, change color, turn.

Row 13: Ch 3, dc in sc, [sk next dc, sc in next dc, sk next dc, 3 dc in next sc] across, ending row with sk dc, sc in next dc, sk next dc, 2 dc in last sc, change color, turn.

Row 14: Ch 1, [sc in next dc, sk next dc, 3 dc in next sc, sk next dc] across, ending row with sc into dc, sk next dc, 2 dc in next sc, hdc in next dc, change color, turn.

Row 15: Ch 1, sk hdc, [sc in next dc, sk next dc, 3 dc in next sc, sk next dc] across, ending row with sc in dc, sk next dc, 2 dc in last sc, change color, turn.

Row 16: Ch 1, [sc in next dc, sk next dc, 3 dc in next sc, sk next dc] across, ending row with sc in dc, sk next dc, 2 dc in next sc, change color, turn. *(15 [19, 23, 23, 27] sts)* Continue even until piece measures the same as back to shoulder, fasten off.

Right Front

Work the same as left front reversing all shaping.

Sleeve

Make 2.

With A, ch 38 [38, 46, 46, 46], beg shell pattern color sequence, work even on 37 [37, 45, 45, 45] sts for 2 rows, change color, turn.

Inc row (RS): Ch 3, (dc, sc) in first dc, [sk next dc, 3 dc in next sc, sk next dc, sc in next dc] across, ending row with sk next dc, 3 dc in next sc, sk next dc, (sc, 2 dc) in top of beg ch, change color, turn.

Inc 2 sts each side every 4th row 1 [2, 3, 4, 5] times, then every 6th row 6 [5, 4, 3, 2] times. *(69 [69, 77, 77, 77] sts)*

Continue even until sleeve measures approximately 21 [20½, 20, 20, 19] inches from beg, fasten off.

CONTINUED ON PAGE 62 ▶

Night on the Town

Soft, velvety pink chenille yarn highlighted with lustrous antique-gold nylon cord and dainty gold beads create the vintage look of this elegant evening purse.

DESIGN BY
RUTH SHEPHERD

Intermediate ●●●

Size
7¼ inches long, excluding tassel

Materials
- Elmore-Pisgah Honeysuckle bulky (chunky) weight yarn art. 810 (88 yds per ball):
    88 yds #9 rose
- 3 oz #18 tan nylon cord
- Size F/5/3.75mm crochet hook or size needed to obtain gauge
- Tapestry needle
- Beading needle
- Sewing needle
- Thread to match fabric
- 17 x 18-inch lining fabric
- ¾-inch gold metal ring: 3
- 4mm gold beads: 10

Gauge
Rnd 4 of motif, 4 sc = 1 inch; motif = 3 inches square
Check gauge to save time.

Pattern Notes
Weave in loose ends as work progresses.
Join rounds with a slip stitch unless otherwise stated.

Motif
Make 10.
Rnd 1 (RS): With rose, ch 5, sl st in first ch to form a ring, ch 2 *(counts as first hdc throughout)*, 7 hdc in ring, join in 2nd ch of beg ch-2. *(8 hdc)*

CONTINUED ON PAGE 63 ▶

Diamond Lace

DESIGN BY
CAROL CARLILE

Intermediate •••

Size
17 x 75 inches, excluding fringe

Materials
- Aunt Lydia's crochet cotton size 10 (400 yds per ball):
  - 1,700 yds #0001 white
- Size 5/1.90mm steel crochet hook or size needed to obtain gauge
- Beading needle
- 6mm crystal beads: 154

A trellised pattern of openwork diamonds and sparkling beaded fringe combine for a dazzling look in this light, lacy shawl that's the perfect finishing touch for an evening outfit.

Gauge
[Dc in next st, ch 2, sk 2 sts] 4 times *(4 sps)* = 1¼ inches; 4 rows of sps = 1¼ inches
Check gauge to save time.

Pattern Notes
Weave in loose ends as work progresses.
Join rounds with a slip stitch unless otherwise stated.

Shawl
Row 1: Ch 156, dc in 4th ch from hook, dc in each of next 2 chs, [ch 2, sk each of next 2 chs, dc in next ch *(space)*, dc in each of next 3 chs *(block)*] 25 times, turn. *(26 blocks; 25 sps)*
Row 2: Ch 5 *(counts as first dc, ch 2 throughout)*, sk each of next 2 sts, dc in next st, [2 dc in next ch-2 sp, dc in next st, ch 2, sk each of next 2 sts, dc in next st] across, turn.
Row 3: Ch 3 *(counts as first dc throughout)*, 2 dc in ch-2 sp, dc in next dc, [ch 2, sk each of next 2 sts, dc in next st] 49 times, 2 dc in next ch-2 sp, dc in next dc, turn. *(1 block; 49 sps; 1 block)*
Row 4: Ch 5, sk each of next 2 sts, dc in next st, 2 dc in next ch-2 sp, dc in next dc, [ch 2, sk each of next 2 sts, dc in next st] 23 times, 2 dc

in next ch-2 sp, dc in next st, [ch 2, sk each of next 2 sts, dc in next st] 23 times, 2 dc in next ch-2 sp, dc in next st, ch 2, sk each of next 2 sts, dc in next st, turn. *(1 sp; 1 block; 23 sps; 1 block; 23 sps; 1 block; 1 sp)*
Rows 5–24: Following graph *(see page 48)* for Rows 5–24, working blocks and sps as indicated.
Rows 25–206: Follow graph for Rows 25–38, until a total of 13 rep are completed.
Rows 207–231: Follow graph for Rows 207–231. At the end of row 231, fasten off.

Edging
Note: *Thread 154 crystal beads onto white cotton.*
Rnd 1: Working across long edge, attach white in any corner, ch 1, *[2 sc over side edge of each dc row and 3 sc over side edge of each row that begins with a ch-5 *(5 sc over each 2-row group)*] across long edge *(587 sc)*, working across short end of shawl, [ch 40, drop lp from hook, push up bead close to dropped lp, insert hook in opposite side of bead and pick up dropped lp and draw through bead, sk next st on shawl, sl st in next st] across edge *(77 beaded ch lps)*, rep from * around, join in beg sc, fasten off. ◆

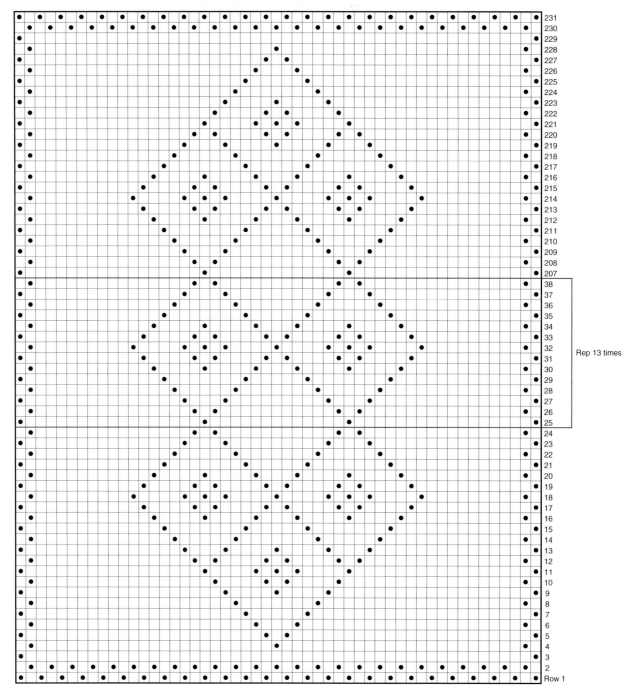

Diamond Lace Chart

Rep 13 times

Bubblegum Flash

DESIGNS BY
SUE COLLINS OTTINGER

Soft, feathery yarn in a fanciful splash of bright bubblegum colors gives a fun look to this little girls' crocheted purse and hat set, complete with purchased gloves trimmed to match.

Easy ●●

Size
Child's hat sizes 4 [8]
Pattern is written for smallest size with changes for larger in brackets.
Purse: 4 x 7 inches

Materials
- Patons Twister super bulky (super chunky) weight yarn (1.75 oz/47 yds/50g per skein):
   2 skeins #5711 fruit loops
- Medium (worsted) weight yarn (3½ oz/205 yds/85g per skein):
   3 oz black
- Sizes F/5/3.75mm, G/6/4mm and P/15mm crochet hooks or sizes needed to obtain gauge
- Yarn needle
- Purchased stretch knit gloves
- Stitch marker

Gauge
Size P hook: 4 sc = 3 inches
Size G hook: 4 sc = 1 inch; 4 sc rnds = 1 inch
Check gauge to save time.

Pattern Note
Weave in loose ends as work progresses.

Hat
Rnd 1 (RS): With size P hook and fruit loops, ch 2, 9 sc in 2nd ch from hook. *(9 sc)*

CONTINUED ON PAGE 64 ▶

Rainbow Sherbet

DESIGNS BY
MARGARET HUBERT

A colorful mix of confectionery colors in a frothy blend of eyelash and microfiber yarns creates the delicious look of this adorable girls' sweater and matching beret.

Intermediate •••

Size
Sizes 4 [6, 8]
Pattern is written for smallest size with changes for larger in brackets.

Materials
- Patons Cha Cha super bulky (super chunky) weight yarn (1.75 oz/77 yds/50g per skein):
  7 [8, 9] skeins #2004 salsa
- Patons Astra light (light worsted) weight yarn (1.75 oz/133 yds/50g per skein):
  1 [1, 2] skeins #8714 mango
- Sizes G/6/4mm and J/10/6mm crochet hooks or sizes needed to obtain gauge
- Yarn needle
- ¾-inch shank buttons: 5
- Stitch markers
- Straight pins

Gauge
Size J hook: 9 sts = 4 inches
Size G hook: 7 sc = 2 inches
Check gauge to save time.

Pattern Notes
Weave in loose ends as work progresses.
Join rounds with a slip stitch unless otherwise stated.

Sweater

Back
Row 1 (RS): With size J hook and salsa, ch 36 [38, 40] loosely, dc in 4th ch from hook, dc in each rem ch across, turn. *(34 [36, 38] dc)*
Row 2: Ch 3 *(counts as first dc throughout)*, dc in each dc across, turn.
Rep row 2 until back measures 8½ [9, 9½] inches. Place a st marker for armhole at each end of row.
Rep row 2 until from beg back measures 14 [15, 16] inches, fasten off.

Left Front
Row 1 (RS): With size J hook and salsa, ch 18 [19, 20] loosely, dc in 4th ch from hook, dc in each rem ch across, turn. *(16 [17, 18] dc)*
Row 2: Ch 3, dc in each dc across, turn.

Rep row 2 until back measures 8½ [9, 9½] inches. Place a st marker at outer edge.
Rep row 2 until front measures 12 [13, 14] inches, ending at armhole edge.

Neck shaping
Row 1: Ch 3, dc in each of next 10 [11, 12] dc, turn leaving rem 5 [5, 5] dc unworked. *(11 [12, 13] dc)*
Row 2: Sl st in next st, ch 3, dc in each rem dc across, turn. *(10 [11, 12] dc)*
Row 3: Ch 3, dc in each of next 8 [9, 10] dc, turn. *(9 [10, 11] dc)*
Row 4: Ch 3, dc in each dc across, turn.
Rep row 4 until front measures the same as back, fasten off.

Right Front
Rep as for left front to neck shaping, ending at neckline edge, turn. *(16 [17, 18] dc)*

Neck shaping
Row 1: Sl st in each of next 5 [5, 5] dc, sl st in next dc, ch 3, dc in each rem dc across, turn. *(11 [12, 13] dc)*
Row 2: Ch 3, dc in each of next 9 [10, 11] dc, turn. *(10 [11, 12] dc)*
Row 3: Sl st in next dc, ch 3, dc in each rem dc across, turn. *(9 [10, 11] dc)*
Row 4: Ch 3, dc in each dc across, turn.

CONTINUED ON PAGE 65 ▶

Hand-Paint Medley

DESIGN BY
MARGRET WILLSON

Deep jewel tones combine in perfect harmony to paint the rich color palette of this luxurious mohair-blend cardigan elegantly trimmed with lacy collar and jeweled buttons.

Intermediate ●●●

Size

Small, [medium, large, extra-large, extra-extra-large]

Finished bust: 39 [43, 47, 51, 55] inches

Back length: 23 [23¾, 24¾, 24¾, 25½] inches

Pattern is written for smallest size with changes for larger in brackets.

Materials

• Brown Sheep Handpaint medium (worsted) weight yarn (1.75 oz/88 yds/50g per hank):
    18 [19, 21, 23, 25] hanks #HP100 mountain majesty
    2 hanks #HP55 ink blue
• Size I/9/5.5mm crochet hook or size needed to obtain gauge
• Yarn needle
• ¾-inch novelty shank buttons: 6

Gauge

(Sc, dc) 6 times = 4 inches; 14 rows = 4 inches
Check gauge to save time.

Pattern Notes

Weave in loose ends as work progresses.

Row 2 establishes pattern.

At the ends of rows and within pattern when referring to a group, a group is (sc, dc) in same stitch.

Back

Row 1 (RS): With mountain majesty, ch 92 [101, 110, 119, 128], (sc, dc) in 2nd ch from hook, sk next 2 chs, *(sc, dc) in next ch, sk next 2 chs, rep from * across to last ch, sc in last ch, turn. *(30 [33, 36, 39, 42] groups)*

Row 2: Ch 1, (sc, dc) in each sc across to last sc, ending with sc in last sc, turn.

Rows 3–51: Rep row 2. At the end of row 51 fasten off, turn.

Underarm shaping

Row 52: Sk 3 [4, 4, 4, 5] groups, attach mountain majesty in next sc, rep row 2 across leaving last 3 [4, 4, 4, 5] groups unworked. *(24 [25, 28, 31, 32] groups)*

Rows 53–81 [53–85, 53–87, 53–89]: Rep row 2 of pattern. Fasten off at the end of last rep.

Right Front

Row 1 (RS): With mountain majesty, ch 47 [50, 56, 59, 65], (sc, dc) in 2nd ch from hook, sk next 2 chs, *(sc, dc) in next ch, sk next 2 chs, rep from * across, ending with sc in last ch, turn.

Row 2: Ch 1, (sc, dc) in each sc across to last sc, ending with sc in last sc, turn.

Rows 3–51: Rep row 2. At the end of row 51, fasten off, turn.

Underarm shaping

Row 52: Sk first 3 [4, 4, 4, 5] groups, attach mountain majesty in next sc, rep row 2 across, turn. *(12 [12, 14, 15, 16] groups)*

Rows 53–69 [53–71, 53–73, 53–75, 53–75]: Rep row 2 of pattern, ending with a RS row.

Neck shaping

Row 70 [72, 74, 76, 76]: Rep row 2 across 9 [9, 11, 12, 13] groups, turn, leaving rem 3 groups unworked.

Row 71–76 [73–78, 75–80, 77–82, 77–84]: Working in pattern of row 2, **sc dec** *(see Stitch Guide)* in next 2 sts at neck edge each of next 6 [6, 6,

6, 8] rows. (6 [6, 8, 9, 9] groups)

Rows 77–81 [79–83, 81–85, 83–87, 85–89]: Rep row 2. At the end of last rep, fasten off.

Left Front

Rows 1–51: Rep rows 1–51 of right front. At the end of row 51, do not fasten off.

Row 52: Work in pattern of row 2, work across 12 [12, 14, 15, 16] groups, leaving rem 3 [4, 4, 4, 5] groups unworked, turn.

Rows 53–69 [53–71, 53–73, 53–75, 53–75]: Work even in pattern of row 2. At the end of last rep, fasten off.

Neck shaping

Row 70 [72, 74, 76, 76]: Sk first 3 groups, attach mountain majesty in next sc, work row 2 of pattern across rem 9 [9, 11, 12, 13] groups, turn.

Rows 71–76 [73–78, 75–80, 77–82, 77–84]: Working in pattern of row 2, sc dec in next 2 sts at neck edge each of next 6 [6, 6, 6, 8] rows. (6 [6, 8, 9, 9] groups)

Rows 77–81 [79–83, 81–85, 83–87, 85–89]: Rep row 2. At the end of last rep, fasten off.

Sleeve

Make 2.

Row 1: With mountain majesty, ch 44 [44, 44, 50, 50], (sc, dc) in 2nd ch from hook, sk next 2 chs, *(sc, dc) in next ch, sk next 2 chs, rep from * across, ending with sc in last

ch, turn. (14 [14, 14, 16, 16] groups)

Rows 2–66 [2–64, 2–64, 2–64, 2–62]: Work in row 2 established pattern, inc 1 sc each end of row every 2 rows 0 [0, 8, 8, 10] times, then every 3 rows 6 [13, 8, 8, 8] times, then every 4 rows 6 [1, 0, 0, 0] times incorporating new sts into pattern. (26 [28, 30, 32, 34] groups)

Rows 67–73 [65–73, 65–73, 65–73, 63–73]: Rep row 2 of established pattern. At the end of last rep, fasten off.

Assembly

Sew shoulder seams, fold sleeve in half, place center top of sleeve at shoulder seam, sew last row of sleeve into arm opening and side edge of rows of sleeve to underarm shaping *(side edge of rows of sleeve are sewn to the 3 [4, 4, 4, 5] sk groups of underarm shaping)*, sew side and sleeve seams.

Edging

Row 1 (RS): Attach ink blue at lower right front corner, ch 1, work 76 [78, 80, 80, 82] sc up edge to beg of neck shaping, 3 sc in next corner, sc evenly around neck opening to left front corner, 3 sc in corner, 76 [78, 80, 80, 82] sc evenly sp down left front to lower left corner, turn.

Row 2: Ch 1, sc in each sc across, turn.

Row 3 (buttonhole row): Ch 1, sc

in each of next 3 [4, 2, 2, 3] sc, ch 3, sk next 3 sc, {sc in each of next 11 [11, 12, 12, 12] sc, ch 3, sk next 3 sc} 5 times, sc in each sc to corner sc, 3 sc in corner, sc in each sc to left front corner, 3 sc in corner sc, sc in each sc down left front, turn.

Row 4: Ch 1, sc in each sc and each ch across, turn.

Row 5: Ch 1, [sc in each sc to next center corner sc, 3 sc in center corner sc] twice, sc in each rem sc down left front, fasten off.

Sew buttons opposite buttonholes.

Collar

Row 1 (RS): Beg at right front neck corner, sk corner sc, sk next 3 sc, attach ink blue in next sc, ch 3 *(counts as first dc)*, *2 dc in next sc, dc in next sc, rep from * around neck edge leaving last 3 sts and corner sc at left front corner unworked, turn.

Rows 2–6: Ch 3 *(counts as first dc)*, dc in each dc across, turn. At the end of row 6, fasten off.

Collar edging

With RS facing, attach ink blue at base of collar on left front, working evenly around entire edge of collar, around ends of rows on side edges and in each st across length of collar, ch 1, sc in first st, *(sc, ch 3, sc) in next st, sc in next st, rep from * across, ending at base of collar on right front edge, fasten off. ◆

Pearls in the Snow

DESIGNS BY
KIM GUZMAN

This pretty, pristine scarf and hat set, accented with lustrous pearl bead edgings, works up quickly and easily with a double-ended crochet hook and medium yarn.

Gauge

Size H hook: 4 sts = 1 inch;
Size K hook: 5 sts = 1½ inches
Check gauge to save time.

Pattern Notes

Weave in loose ends as work progresses.

Join rounds with a slip stitch unless otherwise stated.

Remaining loop on hook counts as first stitch of following row.

Special Stitches

Afghan stitch (afghan st): When opening sts in afghan st, retaining all lps on hook and working right to left, insert hook under front vertical bar, yo, draw up a lp.

Reverse afghan stitch (reverse afghan st): When opening sts for a reverse afghan st, place hook behind work, retaining all lps on hook, insert hook in the back vertical bar, yo, draw up a lp. This makes a firm ridge on the right side of work.

Hat

Row 1 (RS): With size H hook, ch 35, working in the back bar of each ch, beg in 2nd ch from hook, draw up a lp in each rem ch across (*35 lps*

on hook), do not fasten off, attach a 2nd skein with a sl st and draw through the first lp on hook, *yo, draw through 2 lps on hook, rep from * across until 1 lp remains on hook.

Row 2: Work 34 **reverse afghan sts** *(see Special Stitches)* across, drop yarn from this skein, do not fasten off, turn work and pick up yarn from the first skein, yo and draw through 1 lp, *yo, draw through 2 lps, rep from * across until 1 lp remains on hook.

Row 3: Work 34 **afghan sts** *(see Special Stitches)* across, drop yarn from this skein, do not fasten off, turn work and pick up yarn from the 2nd skein, yo and draw through 1 lp, *yo, draw through 2 lps on hook, rep from * across until 1 lp remains on hook.

Row 4: Work 29 reverse afghan sts across, leaving rem 5 sts unworked, drop yarn from this skein, do not fasten off, turn work and pick up yarn from the first skein, yo, draw through 1 lp, *yo, draw through 2 lps on hook, rep from * across until 1 lp remains on hook.

Row 5: Work 29 afghan sts across, drop yarn from this skein, turn work and working with the 2nd skein,

Intermediate •••

Size

Hat: 24 inches in diameter
Scarf: 7½ x 48 inches, excluding
    fringe

Materials

- Red Heart TLC medium (worsted) weight yarn:
  (5 oz/372 yds/141g per skein):
    5 skeins #5001 white
- Sizes H/8/5mm and K/10½/ 6.5mm double-ended crochet hooks or sizes needed to obtain gauge
- Yarn needle
- Sewing needle
- White thread
- 6mm round gray pearl beads: 81
- 3 x 9-inch piece cardboard

yo, draw through 1 lp, *yo, draw through 2 lps on hook, rep from * across until 1 lp remains on hook.

Row 6: Work 24 reverse afghan sts across leaving 5 sts unworked, drop yarn, turn and working with first skein, yo, draw through 1 lp, *yo, draw through 2 lps on hook, rep from * across until 1 lp remains on hook.

Row 7: Work 24 afghan sts across, drop yarn, turn and working with 2nd skein, yo, draw through first lp on hook, *yo, draw through 2 lps on hook, rep from * across until 1 lp remains on hook.

Row 8: Work 19 reverse afghan sts across, leaving rem 5 sts unworked, drop yarn, turn and working with first skein, yo, draw through first lp, *yo, draw through 2 lps on hook, rep from * across until 1 lp remains on hook.

Row 9: Work 19 afghan sts across, drop yarn, turn and working with 2nd skein, yo, draw through first lp on hook, *yo, draw through 2 lps on hook, rep from * across until 1 lp remains on hook.

Row 10: Picking up lps in the unworked sts from rows below, work 34 reverse afghan sts across, drop yarn, turn and working with first skein, yo, draw through first lp on hook, *yo, draw through 2 lps on hook, rep from * across until 1 lp remains on hook.

Row 11: Work 34 afghan sts across, drop yarn, turn and working with 2nd skein, yo, draw through first lp on hook, *yo, draw through 2 lps

on hook, rep from * across until 1 lp remains on hook.

Rows 12–111: [Rep rows 2–11] 10 times.

Rows 112–120: Rep rows 2–10.

Row 121: Working in afghan st, [insert hook in st, yo, draw up a lp and draw through st on hook] across, leaving an 18-inch length of yarn, fasten off. Fasten off rem skein at opposite edge and secure. Thread yarn needle with rem length of yarn, with WS facing, st tog the first row and the last row along edge to top, knot to secure and weave rem length through top edge, draw opening closed and secure, fasten off.

Tassel

Cut 2 lengths of yarn each 12 inches long and set aside. Wind yarn around the 9-inch edge of cardboard 15 times. Tie top edge of tassel with a 12-inch length of yarn. Cut strands of yarn at bottom edge of tassel and remove from cardboard. Tie rem 12-inch length of yarn approximately ¾ inch below top tie. Attach tassel to center top of hat, trim ends evenly.

Beadwork

With sewing needle and thread, sew 51 beads evenly spaced around bottom edge of hat.

Scarf

Row 1: With size K hook, ch 160, insert hook in 2nd ch from hook,

yo, draw up a lp, [insert hook in next ch, yo, draw up a lp] across *(160 lps on hook)*, attach a 2nd skein of yarn with a sl st, yo, draw through first lp on hook, *yo, draw through 2 lps on hook, rep from * across until 1 lp remains, remains lp on hook counts as first st on following row.

Row 2: Work 159 afghan sts across, drop yarn, turn, working with the first skein, yo, draw through first lp on hook, *yo, draw through 2 lps on hook, rep from * across until 1 lp remains on hook.

Row 3: Work 159 afghan sts across, drop yarn, turn, working with the 2nd skein, yo, draw through first lp on hook, *yo, draw through 2 lps on hook, rep from * across until 1 lp remains on hook.

Rows 4–27: [Rep rows 2 and 3] 12 times.

Row 28: *Insert hook in next st, yo, draw up a lp and draw through st on hook, rep from * across, fasten off.

Fringe

Wind yarn around the 9-inch edge of cardboard, cut bottom edge of strands. Attach fringe on each end of scarf across short edges. Fold 2 strands in half, insert hook in edge of row, draw strands through at fold to form a lp on hook, draw cut ends through lp on hook, pull ends gently to secure. Work 15 groups of fringe across each short edge of scarf. Trim ends evenly. ◆

foundation ch at center of front, ch 1, sc in same ch, *ch 1, sk 1 row (or ch-1 sp on sides), sc in end of next row (or in next sc on sides)*, rep from * to * around, working at each corner, ch 1, sk 1 row (or 1 ch-1 sp), (sc, ch 2, sc) in corner sc, at end of rnd, ch 1, sk last row, join in beg sc, sl st in next ch-1 sp.

Rnd 2 (RS): Ch 4 (counts as first dc, ch 1), sk next sc, dc in next ch-1 sp, *ch 1, sk next sc, dc in next ch-1 sp*, rep from * to * around, working at each corner, ch 1, sk next sc, (dc, ch 1, dc, ch 2, dc, ch 1, dc) in corner ch-2 sp, at end of rnd, ch 1, sk last sc, join in 3rd ch of beg ch-4, fasten off, turn.

Rnd 3 (WS): Draw up a lp of navy fleck in 3rd ch-1 sp to the left of corner ch-2 sp on either side edge, ch 1*, rep from * to * around working at each corner, ch 1, sk next dc, (sc, ch 2, sc) in corner ch-2 sp, at end of rnd, ch 1, sk last dc, join in beg sc, turn.

Note: On the following round, sk over sc sts and work in ch-1 sps and corner ch-2 sps only.

Rnd 4 (RS): Ch 1, (sc, ch 2, sc) in each ch-1 sp around and (sc, ch 2, sc, ch 4, sc, ch 2, sc) in each corner ch-2 sp, join in beg sc, fasten off.

Back

Rep same as for front and work border through rnd 2. At end of rnd 2, fasten off.

Mark edge to join and edge for button lps, then work border rnd 3. On rnd 4, join corner ch-4 sp and next 28 ch-2 sps and next corner ch-4 sp to appropriate end of front piece and make button lps on appropriate end of 2nd piece as specified. Continue in pattern st, to join corners, ch 2, drop lp, draw lp under to over through opposite ch-4 sp, ch 2 and continue. To join next 28 ch-2 sps, ch 1, drop lp, draw lp under to over through opposite ch-2 sp, ch 1 and continue. To join last corner, ch 1, drop lp, draw lp under to over through opposite ch-4 sp, ch

1 and continue pattern all around to next corner.

Button loop edge

Working from top neck edge to bottom, the first button lp is the corner ch-4 sp, (sc, ch 2, sc) in next 2 ch-1 sps, [(sc, ch 4, sc) in next ch-1 sp, (sc, ch 2, sc) in each of next 3 ch-1 sps] 6 times, working final corner, (sc, ch 4, sc, ch 4, sc, ch 2, sc), then continue pattern around to end. (8 button lps)

With a length of navy fleck, sew buttons opposite button lps.

Neckline tie

Holding 2 strands of navy fleck tog, leaving a 5-inch length at beg, ch 150, leaving a 5-inch length, fasten off. Beg at center front, weave over and under ch-1 sps of rnd 3 at neckline edge around to opposite edge of front neckline edge.

For each end of tie, cut 3 strands navy fleck 10 inches long and draw through end of ch, tie with tails in an overhand knot and trim as desired. ◆

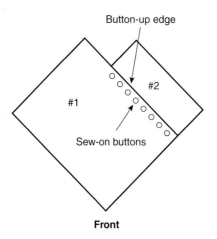

Front

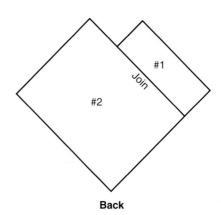

Back

Casual Stripes CONTINUED FROM PAGE 22 ▶

1–136]: Rep the same as back body in pattern row and striping sequence ending with pattern row 2.

First neck shaping

Row 115 (121, 125, 131, 137): Ch 1, 2 sc in first sc, sk next dc, [(sc, ch 2, sc) in next sc, sk next dc] 15 [17, 19, 21, 22] times, 2 sc in next sc, turn.

Rows 116–122 [122–128, 126–132, 132–138, 138–144]: Working in pattern rows, **sc dec** *(see Stitch Guide)* in next 2 sts at neck edge every RS row 4 times, turn.

Rows 123–132 [129–138, 133–142, 139–148, 145–154]: Work in pattern rows on rem 29 [33, 37, 41, 43] sts. At the end of last rep, fasten off.

Second neck shaping

Row 115 [121, 125, 131, 137]: Sk center 29 [29, 31, 33, 37] sts, attach yarn in next st and work in pattern row 3, turn.

Rows 116–132 [122–138, 126–142, 138–154]: Rep first neck shaping.

Sleeve

Make 2.

Ribbing

Row 1 (RS): With slate, ch 51, dc in 4th ch from hook, dc in each rem ch across, turn. *(49 dc)*

Rows 2–11: Rep rows 2–11 of back ribbing.

Body

Rows 1–108: Working in pattern as for back body, increase 1 st each end of row on RS rows every 2 rows 0 [0, 0, 1, 11] times, then every 4 rows 1 [16, 22, 26, 21] times, then every 6 rows 17 [7, 3, 0, 0] times. *(85 [95, 99, 103, 113] sts)* At the same time, with slate work 3 [7, 7, 7, 9] rows, then working color sequence, *2 rows basil, 2 rows café, 2 rows burgundy, 2 rows café, 2 rows basil, 8 [10, 10, 10, 12] rows slate, rep from * 5 [4, 4, 4, 4] more times, 2 rows basil, 2 rows café, 2 rows burgundy, 2 rows café and 2 rows basil, then work 5 [11, 11, 11, 11] rows slate, ending with pattern row 2, fasten off.

Assembly

Sew shoulder seams. For sleeve placement, measure down from shoulder seam on front and back each side 9 [10, 10½, 11, 12] inches and mark with st markers. Matching center of last row of sleeve to shoulder seam, sew sleeve between markers to body. Sew sleeve and side seams.

Neckline Ribbing

Rnd 1 (RS): Attach slate at right shoulder seam, ch 3 *(counts as first dc)*, work 109 [109, 113, 117, 125] dc evenly sp around neckline opening, join in 3rd ch of beg ch-3. *(110 [110, 114, 118, 126] dc)*

Rnd 2: Ch 2 *(counts as first hdc)*, [fpdc around next st, bpdc around next st] around, join in 2nd ch of beg ch-2.

Rnds 3–7: Ch 2, [fpdc around fpdc, bpdc around bpdc] around, join in 2nd ch of beg ch-2. At the end of row 7, fasten off. ◆

Crimson Fire CONTINUED FROM PAGE 24 ▶

beg of armhole dec, armhole measures 6½ [7, 7½] inches from beg, ending at center front edge. At neckline edge, sl st over 14 sts, work in pattern across rem sts. Working in pattern, dec 1 st at neck edge every row 6 [6, 4] times. Work in pattern on rem 16 [18, 20] sts until armhole measures the same as back, fasten off. *(16 [18,20] sts)*

Right Front

With size H hook and prairie fire, ch 44 [46, 48] work in pattern the same as for back to armhole, ending at front opening edge. *(44 [46, 48] sts)* To shape armhole, work in pattern across to last 4 [4, 4] sts, do not work rem sts, turn. *(40 [42, 44] sts)* Continue in row 2 of pattern and keeping center front even, dec armhole edge every other row 4 [4, 6] times. *(36 [38, 38] sts)* Work even in pattern until from beg of armhole dec, armhole measures 6½ [7, 7½] inches from beg, ending at armhole edge. Work in pattern across 22 [24, 24] sts, leaving rem 14 [14, 14] sts at neckline edge unworked. Working in pattern, dec 1 st at neck edge every row 6 [6, 4] times. Work in pattern on rem 16 [18, 20] sts until armhole measures the same as back, fasten off. *(16 [18, 20] sts)*

Sleeve
Make 2.
With size H hook and prairie fire, ch 38 [40, 42] work in pattern across row. *(38 [40, 42] sts)* Working in pattern, inc 1 st each side every 2 inches 6 [7, 8] times. *(50 [54, 58] sts)* Work in pattern until sleeve

measures 15½ [16, 16½] inches from beg.
To shape armhole, sl st across 4 [4, 4] sts, work in pattern across row until 4 [4, 4] sts rem, leaving these sts unworked, turn. *(42 [46, 50] sts)* Working in pattern, dec 1 st each edge every other row 4 [4, 4] times (34 [38, 42] sts), then every row 9 [10, 11] times. At the end of last rep, fasten off. *(16 [18, 20] sts)*

Assembly

Sew shoulder seams of back and fronts tog. Fold sleeve in half lengthwise, pin center of sleeve cap to shoulder seam, pin sleeve into armhole opening easing in fullness as needed, sew sleeve in place. Sew sleeve and side seams.

Neckline & Front Trim

Row 1 (RS): With size H hook, attach prairie fire at right front bottom, ch 1, sc evenly sp up front edge, working 3 sc in right top front corner, sc evenly sp around neckline, working 3 sc in left top front corner, sc evenly sp to bottom left ending with the same number of sc sts as on right front, turn.
Row 2 (WS): Ch 1, sc in each sc of row 1, working 3 sc in each center top corner sc, turn.
Note: On right front, starting approximately 9 [9½, 10] inches up from bottom, place first marker for first buttonhole, place rem markers for rem buttonholes.
Row 3 (RS): Ch 1, sc in each sc, working ch 3, sk 2 sts for each buttonhole at each marker and working 3 sc in center top corner, sc around neckline, working 3 sc in center corner sc, sc in each sc down left front, turn.
Row 4 (WS): Ch 1, sc in each sc, working 3 sc in each center corner

sc and 2 sc in each ch-3 sp of each buttonhole, turn.
Row 5 (RS): Rep row 2, do not turn.
Row 6 (RS): Ch 1, reverse sc in each sc, do not work 3 sc in corners, fasten off.

Sleeve Trim

Rnd 1 (RS): With size H hook, attach prairie fire at sleeve seam and working in opposite side of foundation ch, ch 1, reverse sc in each ch around, join in beg sc, fasten off.

Scarf

Row 1: With size K hook and prairie fire, ch 24, (sc, dc) in 2nd ch from hook, sk next ch, *(sc, dc) in next ch, sk next ch, rep from * across, ending with sc in last ch, turn. *(23 sts)*
Row 2: Ch 1, sc in first sc, *(sc, dc) in next dc, sk next sc, rep from * across, ending with sc in last sc, turn. *(24sts)*
Note: When yarn color is not in use, drop at end of row and weave through edge until needed.
Row 3: Draw up a lp of spice, ch 1, sc in first sc, *(sc, dc) in next dc, sk next sc, rep from * across, ending with sc in last sc, turn.
Row 4: Rep row 2.
Row 5: Draw up a lp of prairie fire, rep row 2.
Row 6: Rep row 2.
Rep rows 3–6 until scarf measures 68 inches. At the end of last rep, fasten off.

Fringe

Wrap prairie fire around 8-inch cardboard 4 times, cut bottom edge of strands. Fold 4 strands in half, insert hook in end of scarf, draw strands through at fold to form a lp on hook, draw cut ends through lp on hook, pull gently to secure. Work a fringe a total of 13 times on each end of scarf. Trim ends evenly. ◆

Retro Chic CONTINUED FROM PAGE 28 ▶

Row 4 (RS): Rep row 2 of belt.
Border
Rnd 5 (RS): Rep rnd 5 of belt border.
Assembly
Working in back lps only, whipstitch strips tog side by side across long edge. Fold piece in half so that short edges of strips are tog at top edge, working in back lps only, sew side seams.
Top opening
Rnd 1: Working around top opening with size I hook, attach natural in side seam, ch 1, sc in same st as beg ch-1, [5 sc evenly sp across strip, 3 dc in joining seam of strips] 3 times, 5 sc across next strip, sc in joining at side seam, work 5 sc across next strip, [3 dc in joining seam of strip, 5 sc evenly sp across strip] 3 times, join in beg sc. *(42 sc; 18 dc)*
Rnds 2–6: Ch 1, sc in each st around, join in beg sc. At the end of rnd 6, fasten off.
Handle
Row 1: With size I hook and country blue, ch 93, dc in 4th ch from hook, dc in each rem ch across, fasten off.
Rnd 2: Working around entire outer edge of handle, attach natural with sl st in any st, ch 1, [sl st in next st, ch 1] evenly sp around outer edge, fasten off.
Sew each end of handle to each side of top opening of purse.
Tassels
Make 9.
Attach tassels evenly sp across bottom edge of purse. For each tassel, cut 10-inch length of natural each 16 inches long. Fold strands in half, insert hook in bottom edge of purse, draw strands through at fold to form a lp on hook, draw cut ends through lp on hook, pull ends to secure. ◆

Sailing Away Sweater CONTINUED FROM PAGE 36 ▶

around, join in beg sc, do not turn. *(23 sts)*
Rnd 2: Ch 1, sc in each sc around, join in beg sc. Rep rnd 2 until sleeve measures from beg 10½ [11½, 13] inches. At the end of last rep, turn.
[Ch 1, sl st in next sc] around, ending with last sl st in joining, fasten off.
Sew sleeve and side seam.

Waves
With RS facing, using graph as a guide, attach sunny yellow as indicated with an X on graph under a boat. [Ch 3, sl st in indicated st 2 rows above, ch 3, sl st in indicated st below] across as indicated.
Rep waves under each of the rem boats. Work wave pattern around entire bottom edge of sweater under the lower boats.

Body Band
Rnd 1 (RS): Attach bright blue at center back neck, ch 1, work 12 sc across to shoulder seam, 19 [25, 31] sc evenly sp to neck edge, 3 sc in corner, 25 [29, 35] sc evenly sp down front to corner, 3 sc in corner, sc across opposite side of foundation ch across bottom of sweater, 3 sc in corner, 25 [29, 35] sc evenly sp up opposite front, 3 sc in corner neckline, 19 [25, 31] sc evenly sp to shoulder seam, 11 sc along rem back neck, join in beg sc.
Rnd 2: Ch 2 *(counts as first hdc throughout)*, **fphdc** *(see Special Stitch)* around next sc, [sc in next sc, fphdc around next sc] around, join in 2nd ch of beg ch-2.
Rnd 3: Ch 2, *fphdc around next fphdc **, sc in next sc, rep from * to corner, [fphdc around fphdc, ch 1, sk 1 st, fphdc around next fphdc *(buttonhole)*, work in pattern over next 3 sts] 5 times, continue in pattern around, ending last rep at **, join in 2nd ch of beg ch-2.
Note: Buttonholes do not extend all the way down the front opening of sweater. If you desire buttonholes down front to bottom, make adjustment in number of sts between buttonholes.
Rnd 4: Ch 1, sl st in each st around, working [ch 1, sl st in next st] 4 times at each lower corner, join in beg sl st.
Rnd 5: Working over last sl st rnd *(not in sl sts)*, [ch 1, sl st in next sp] around, ending with ch 1, join with sl st in first ch-1, fasten off.
Rnd 6: With RS facing, attach bright blue with sl st over fphdc of rnd 3 near side seam, sl st over each st of rnd 3, ending with sl st in same st as beg st, fasten off.
Sew buttons opposite buttonholes. ◆

Flowering Vines CONTINUED FROM PAGE 40 ▶

Ch 2, 3 **pc** (see *Special Stitches*) in 2nd ch from hook, fasten off.

Vine
Make a ch approximately 40 inches long, 160 chs, fasten off.

Using photo and diagrams as a guide, pin vine in a swirling pattern with a few lps to shirt. With sewing needle and thread in **backstitch** (*see Special Stitches*), sew vine in place.
Using photo and diagrams as a guide, sew

flowers, flower buds and leaves to shirt or sew as desired. ◆

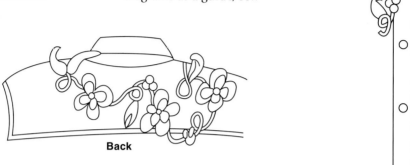

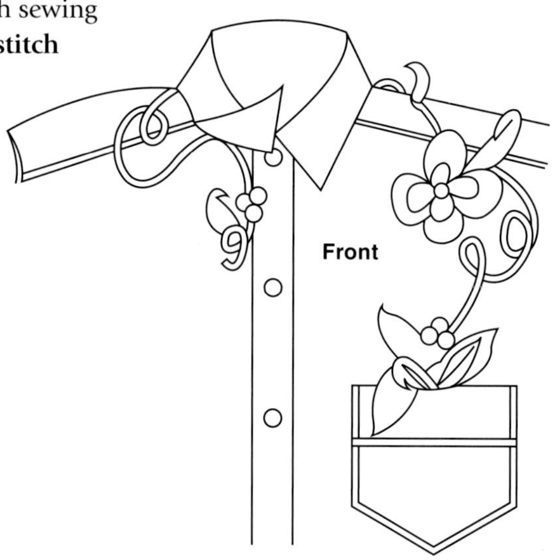

Front

Back

Sophisticated Shells Cardigan CONTINUED FROM PAGE 44 ▶

Finishing
Sew shoulder seams. Set in sleeves, sew sleeve and side seams.

Front Bands
Row 1: With RS facing, attach A with a sl st to right front edge, ch 1, sc evenly along right front, across back

of neck and down left front, turn.
Row 2: Ch 1, sc in each sc, working 2 sc at each side at beg of front neck shaping and **sc dec** (*see Stitch Guide*) each side of back neck shaping, turn. Rep row 2 until band measures approximately ¾ inch.
Place markers for 6 evenly sp buttonholes along right front, making the first ¼ inch from beg of neck

shaping and the last ½ inch from bottom edge.
Continue to rep row 2 and make buttonholes by working (ch 3, sk next 3 sc) where marked. On the following row, work 3 sc in each ch-3 sp of previous row.
Continue in sc as before until band measures 1½ inches, fasten off.
Sew buttons opposite buttonholes. ◆

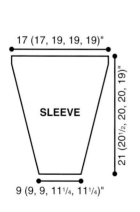

17 (17, 19, 19, 19)"

SLEEVE

21 (20½, 20, 20, 19)"

9 (9, 9, 11¼, 11¼)"

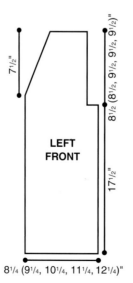

7½"

8½ (8½, 9½, 9½, 9½)"

LEFT FRONT

17½"

8¼ (9¼, 10¼, 11¼, 12¼)"

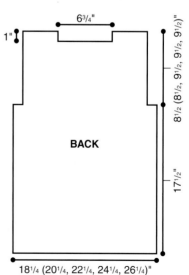

6¾"

1"

8½ (8½, 9½, 9½, 9½)"

BACK

17½"

18¼ (20¼, 22¼, 24¼, 26¼)"

Rnd 2: Ch 1, sc in first st, ch 2, [sc in next st, ch 2] around, join in first sc. *(8 ch sps)*

Rnd 3: Sl st into first ch sp, (ch 2, 2 hdc) in same ch sp, (2 hdc, ch 2, 2 hdc) in next ch sp *(corner made)*, *3 hdc in next ch sp, (2 hdc, ch 2, 2 hdc) in next ch sp, rep from * around, join in top of beg ch-2, fasten off.

Rnd 4: Attach tan in any corner ch-2 sp, ch 1, (sc, ch 2, sc) in same corner ch-2 sp, sc in each of next 7 sts, *(sc, ch 2, sc) in next corner ch-2 sp, sc in each of next 7 sts, rep from * around, join in beg sc, fasten off. *(36 sc; 4 ch-2 sps)*

Rnd 5: Attach nylon cord around post of any st on rnd 2, ch 2, [sl st around post of next st on rnd 2, ch 2] around, join with sl st in first sl st, fasten off.

Using beading needle, sew a bead to center of each motif.

Assembly

For front, sew motifs tog according to front side illustration.

For back, sew motifs tog according to back side illustration, sew side edges of A and B on front side to side edges of A and B on backside. Sew rem edges tog.

Top Band

Rnd 1: Working around top edge, attach tan in any seam, ch 1, sc in same st as beg ch-1, work 59 sc evenly sp around, join in beg sc. *(60 sc)*

Rnd 2: Ch 1, sc in each st around, join in beg sc.

Rnd 3: Ch 4 *(counts as first dc, ch 1)*, sk next st, [dc in next st, ch 1, sk next st] around, join in 3rd ch of beg ch-4.

Rnd 4: Sl st into next ch-1 sp, ch 3, [sl st in next ch-1 sp, ch 3] around, join with sl st in first sl st.

Rnd 5: Rep rnd 4, fasten off.

Drawstring

Make 2.

Holding 1 strand each rose and tan tog, ch 8, sl st in 8th ch from hook, ch 52 or to desired length, sl st in 8th ch from hook, fasten off.

Starting at 1 side edge, weave 1 end of a drawstring through the ch-1 sps of rnd 3 of top band.

Insert ends of drawstring through a gold ring, tie ends into knots. Starting at opposite side, rep with other drawstring.

Fringe

For each fringe, cut 4 strands each 9 inches from rose and tan. Fold strands in half, insert hook from back to front through ch lp, draw fold through to form a lp on hook, draw cut ends through lp on hook, tighten. Trim ends.

Attach fringe in lps on each end of drawstrings.

Tack rem gold ring to center bottom of bag, rep fringe in gold ring.

Lining

Using crochet bag to make a pattern, cut 2 pieces of fabric ½ inch larger on all edges. Sew sides and bottom right sides tog. Place inside crochet piece, fold top edge of fabric ½ inch to WS, sew fold to rnd 2 on top band. ◆

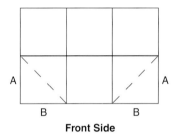

Front Side

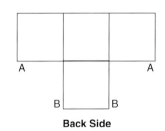

Back Side

Bubblegum Flash CONTINUED FROM PAGE 49 ▶

Rnd 2: [Sc in next sc, ch 1] around. *(18 sts)*

Rnd 3: (Sc, ch 1, sc) in each ch-1 sp around. *(27 sts)*

Rnd 4: Sc in each st around. *(27 sc)*

Note: Size 4 only, rows 5–16, rep rnd 4. At the end of row 16, fasten off. Work rem rnds for size 8.

Rnd 5 (size 8 only): Rep rnd 4.

Rnd 6: 2 sc in first st, sc in each of next 15 sts, 2 sc in next st, sc in each of next 10 sts. *(29 sts)*

Rnd 7: Rep rnd 4. *(29 sts)*

Rnd 8: 2 sc in first st, sc in each of next 16 sts, 2 sc in next st, sc in each of next 11 sts. *(31 sts)*

Rnds 9–20: Rep rnd 4. At the end of rnd 20, sl st in each of next 2 sts, fasten off.

Glove Trim
Make 2.

Rnd 1 (RS): With size F hook and fruit loops, *gently insert hook through top of glove at wrist, yo, draw up a lp large enough for size P hook, remove size F hook and insert size P hook, ch 2, sk 3 ridges on glove **, change back to size F hook, rep from * around, ending last rep at **, sl st to join in beg sc.

Rnd 2: Continuing with size P hook, ch 1, sc in each ch-2 sp around, sl st to join in beg sc, fasten off.

Purse
Rnd 1: With size G hook and black yarn, ch 9, sc in 2nd ch from hook, sc in each of next 6 chs, 3 sc in last ch, working on opposite side of foundation ch, sc in each of next 6 chs, 2 sc in same st as beg sc, do not join rnds, use a st marker. *(18 sc)*

Rnd 2: 2 sc in next sc, sc in each of next 6 sc, 2 sc in each of next 3 sc, sc in each of next 6 sc, 2 sc in each of next 2 sc. *(24 sc)*

Rnd 3: 2 sc in each of next 2 sc, sc in next 7 sc, 2 sc in each of next 5 sc, sc in each of next 7 sc, 2 sc in each of next 3 sc. *(34 sc)*

Rnd 4: Sc in each st around.

Rnd 5: 2 sc in next st, sc in next st, 2 sc in next st, sc in each of next 10 sts, [2 sc in next st, sc in next st] 4 times, sc in each of next 10 sts, 2 sc in next st, sc in next st, 2 sc in last st. *(42 sc)*

Rnd 6: Working in **back lps** *(see Stitch Guide)* for this rnd only, sc in each st around. *(42 sc)*

Rnds 7–29: Rep rnd 4.

Rnd 30: Ch 4 *(counts as first dc, ch 1)*, sk 1 sc, [dc in next sc, ch 1, sk 1 sc] around, sl st to join in 3rd ch of beg ch-4. *(21 dc)*

Rnd 31: [Ch 3, sl st in next dc] around, fasten off.

Rnd 32: With size P hook, attach fruit loops in any ch-3 sp of previous rnd, ch 1, sc in same ch-3 sp, ch 3, [sc in next ch-3 sp, ch 3] around, sl st to join in beg sc, fasten off.

Handle
Make 2.

With size G hook and black, ch 67, fasten off.

Beg at side edge of purse, weave first ch through ch-1 sps of rnd 30 around outer edge, knot ends tog. Beg at opposite side edge of purse, weave 2nd ch through ch-1 sps of rnd 30 around outer edge, knot ends tog. ◆

Rainbow Sherbet CONTINUED FROM PAGE 50 ▶

Rep row 4 until the front measures the same as back, fasten off.

Sleeve
Make 2.

Row 1 (RS): With size J hook and salsa, ch 28 [30, 32] loosely, dc in 4th ch from hook, dc in each rem ch across, turn. *(26 [28, 30] dc)*

Row 2: Ch 3, ch 3, dc in each dc across, turn.

Rows 3–5: Rep row 2.

Row 6: Ch 3, dc in same st as beg ch-3, dc in each dc across to last dc, 2 dc in last dc, turn. *(28 [30, 32] dc)*
(Rep rows 2–6) 3 [3, 3] times. *(34 [36, 38] dc)*

Rep row 2 until sleeve measures 10½ [11, 11½] inches, fasten off.

Assembly
Sew back to fronts across shoulders. Fold last row of sleeve in half, pin center to shoulder seam. Easing in fullness, pin last row of sleeve between armhole markers. Sew side and sleeve seams.

Outer Border
Rnd 1 (RS): With size G hook, attach mango at right side seam *(seam between right front and back of sweater)*, ch 1, working across right front work 25 [27, 29] sc evenly sp across bottom edge to right front corner, 3 sc in corner st, working up right front, work 45 [47, 49] sc to neck edge, 3 sc in corner st, 18 [19, 19] sc across right front neck edge, 22 [24, 26] sc across back neck edge, 18 [19, 19] sc across left front neck edge, 3 sc in corner st, working down left front, work 45 [47, 49] sc, 3 sc in bottom corner st, 25 [27, 29] sc evenly sp across left front bottom edge to side seam, work 50 [54, 58] sc across back of sweater, join in beg sc.

Rnd 2 (RS): Ch 1, sc in each sc around, working 3 sc in each center corner sc, join in beg sc.

Note: For buttonhole markers, place 5 st markers evenly sp up right front of sweater.

Rnd 3 (RS): Ch 1, sc in each sc to center corner sc at bottom right front, 3 sc in corner, [sc up right front to st marker, ch 2, sk 2 sc] 5 times, continue to sc around working 3 sc in each center corner sc around, join in beg sc.

Rnd 4 (RS): Ch 1, sc around, working 3 sc in each corner and 2 sc in each ch-2 sp of each buttonhole, join in beg sc.

Rnd 5 (RS): Rep rnd 2.

Rnd 6 (RS): Ch 1, **reverse sc** *(see illustration)* in each st around, join in beg sc, fasten off.
Sew buttons opposite buttonholes.

Sleeve Trim
Make 2.

Rnd 1 (RS): With size G hook, attach mango at sleeve seam, working in opposite side of foundation ch, ch 1, work 26 [28, 30] sc around, join in beg sc.

Rnd 2 (RS): Ch 1, reverse sc in each sc around, join in beg sc, fasten off.

Hat

Crown
Rnd 1 (RS): With size J hook and salsa, ch 5, sl st to join to form a ring, ch 3 *(does not count as first dc throughout)*, work 8 dc in ring, sl st to join in 3rd ch of beg ch-3. *(8 dc)*

Rnd 2: Ch 3, 2 dc in each dc around, join in 3rd ch of beg ch-3. *(16 dc)*

Rnd 3: Ch 3, [dc in next dc, 2 dc in next dc] around, join in 3rd ch of beg ch-3. *(24 dc)*

Rnd 4: Ch 3, [dc in each of next 2 dc, 2 dc in next dc] around, join in 3rd ch of beg ch-3. *(32 dc)*

Rnd 5: Ch 3, [dc in each of next 3 dc, 2 dc in next dc] around, join in 3rd ch of beg ch-3. *(40 dc)*

Rnd 6: Ch 3, [dc in each of next 4 dc, 2 dc in next dc] around, join in 3rd ch of beg ch-3. *(48 dc)*

Rnd 7: Ch 3, [dc in each of next 5 dc, 2 dc in next dc] around, join in 3rd ch of beg ch-3. *(56 dc)*

Rnd 8: Ch 3, [dc in each of next 6 dc, 2 dc in next dc] around, join in 3rd ch of beg ch-3. *(64 dc)*

Rnds 9–12 [9–14, 9–14]: Ch 3, dc in each dc around, join in 3rd ch of beg ch-3. At the end of last rep, fasten off.

Hat Ribbing
Rnd 1 (RS): With size G hook, attach mango in any dc of last rnd of crown, ch 1, sc in each dc around, join in beg sc. *(64 sc)*

Rnds 2–5: Ch 1, sc in each sc around, join in beg sc.

Rnd 6: Ch 1, reverse sc in each sc around, join in beg sc, fasten off.

Tassel
Make 9.

With size G hook and mango, cut a 16-inch length, fold strand at center and attach center of strand to center top of hat, insert hook into hat near attachment of strand and from center start chaining outward to end of half of the strand, insert hook back at center in first ch of previous section, start chaining outward on the 2nd half of the strand to the end of strand. Rep until all strands are attached to center top of hat. ◆

Crochet for Fun

Crochet can be an important part of our recreational activities, whether we're crocheting simply to relax and unwind or stitching an array of handy accessories that make our fun time even better. In this chapter, you'll find an enticing variety of projects that are sure to add comfort, convenience and enjoyment to play time, vacation, hobbies and travel.

Two-in-One Games

DESIGNS BY
ROSANNE KROPP

Road trips will be twice the fun with this cute-as-a-bug game tote that features checkers on one side and tic-tac-toe on the other. It's easy to carry along, and all the pieces store inside!

Easy ••

Size
Tote: 14 inches square

Materials
- Red Heart Classic medium (worsted) weight yarn (3 oz/174 yds/85g per skein):
   8 oz #848 skipper blue
   3½ oz #261 maize
   2 oz each #676 emerald green and #230 yellow
   ½ oz each #902 jockey red, #245 orange and #12 black
- Size G/6/4mm crochet hook or size needed to obtain gauge
- Yarn needle
- Sewing needle
- Black thread
- Fiberfill
- 10mm sew-on wiggly eyes: 11 pairs
- ¾-inch plastic ring: 24
- 3mm black chenille stem: 2 inches
- ¼-inch red purchased pompoms: 2
- Hot-glue gun
- Stitch marker

Gauge
7 sc = 2 inches; 7 sc rows = 2 inches

Pattern Notes
Weave in loose ends as work progresses.

Join rounds with a slip stitch unless otherwise stated.

Tic-Tac-Toe Game Pieces

Head
Make 5 with jockey red heads and yellow bodies and 5 with orange heads and emerald green bodies.

Rnd 1 (RS): With head color, ch 2, 6 sc in 2nd ch from hook, join in beg sc. *(6sc)*

Rnd 2: Ch 1, 2 sc in each sc around, join in beg sc. *(12 sc)*

Rnd 3: Ch 1, [sc in next sc, 2 sc in next sc] 6 times, join in beg sc. *(18 sc)*

Rnd 4: Working in **front lps** *(see Stitch Guide)* only, [4 sc in next sc, sl st in next sc] twice, fasten off.

Body Top
Note: *Work in **back lps** (see Stitch Guide) only throughout body top.*

Row 1: Now working in rows, sk next 9 sc after last sl st of rnd 4, attach body color, ch 1, sc in same st as beg ch-1, sc in each of next 13 sts, leaving last 4 sc unworked, turn. *(14 sc)*

Row 2: Ch 1, sc in each st across, turn.

Rows 3–8: Rep row 2.

Row 9: Ch 1, sc in first st, [**sc dec** *(see Stitch Guide)* in next 2 sts, sc in next st] 4 times, sc in next st, turn. *(10 sc)*

Row 10: Ch 1, sc in each st across, turn.

Row 11: Ch 1, [sc dec in next 2 sts] 5 times, fasten off. *(5 sc)*

Body Bottom & Legs
Working tightly, with body color, ch 9, 4 dc in 4th ch from hook, *ch 3, sc in 2nd ch from hook, sc in next ch, sl st in top of last dc *(leg completed)*, [2 dc in each of next 2 chs, ch 3, sc in 2nd ch from hook, sc in next ch, sl st in top of last dc] twice*, 5 dc in last ch; working on opposite side of foundation ch, rep from * to * once, sl st to join in 9th ch of beg ch-9, leaving a length of yarn, fasten off. *(26 dc; 6 legs)*

Assembly
Line up body bottom and body sts with first 4 dc of body bottom to rem 4 sts of rnd 3 of head and opposite end 5 dc to end 5 sc of row 11 of body top. Holding legs forward *(do not sew legs)*, sew body

bottom to body top, stuffing lightly with fiberfill before closing. With sewing needle and black thread, sew eyes to upper portion of head over rnd 2.

Checkerboard Game Pieces

Make 12 each jockey red and black checkers.

Rnd 1: Attach yarn to plastic ring, ch 1, 12 sc over ring, join in first sc, fasten off. *(12 sc)*

Caterpillar Head

Note: Do not join rnds; use st marker to mark rnds.

Rnd 1: With yellow, ch 2, 6 sc in 2nd ch from hook. *(6 sc)*

Rnd 2: 2 sc in each sc around. *(12 sc)*

Rnd 3: [Sc in next sc, 2 sc in next sc] 6 times. *(18 sc)*

Rnds 4 & 5: Sc in each sc around.

Rnd 6: [Sc dec in next 2 sc, sc in next sc] 6 times. *(12 sc)*

Rnd 7: [Sc dec in next 2 sc] 6 times, sl st in next st, do not fasten off; stuff head with fiberfill. *(6 sc)*

CONTINUED ON PAGE 109 ▶

Double-Decker Card Set

DESIGNS BY
JENNIFER MOIR

Pretty single and double-deck card holders, stitched in size 10 thread and accented with dainty flowers, add a fun, feminine touch to the ladies' bridge club get-together.

Intermediate ●●●

Size

Single deck case: ¾ x 4 inches
Double deck case: 1½ x 4 inches

Materials

- South Maid crochet cotton size 10 (350 yds per ball):
    1 ball #480 delft
    25 yds #482 true blue
    5 yds #484 myrtle green
- Size 7/1.65mm steel crochet hook or size needed to obtain gauge
- Tapestry needle
- 10mm blue novelty buttons: 2
- Stitch markers: 4

Gauge

4 shells = 1¾ inches; 6 shell rnds = 1½ inches
Check gauge to save time.

Pattern Notes

Weave in loose ends as work progresses.
Join rounds with a slip stitch unless otherwise stated.

Special Stitches

Shell: (2 dc, ch 2, 2 dc) in indicated st.
Beginning shell (beg shell): (Ch 3, dc, ch 2, 2 dc) in indicated st.
Front post double crochet (fpdc): Yo, insert hook front to back to front again around vertical post of indicated st, yo, draw up a lp, (yo, draw through 2 lps on hook] twice.
Picot: Ch 3, sl st in top of last st.

Single-Deck Case

Base

Row 1: With delft, ch 26, hdc in 3rd ch from hook, hdc in each rem ch across, turn. *(25 hdc)*

Row 2: Ch 2 *(counts as first hdc throughout)*, hdc in each hdc across, turn.

Rows 3 & 4: Rep row 2. At the end of row 4, do not turn.

Rnd 5: Now working in rnds, ch 1, work 7 sc evenly sp across ends of rows, 3 sc in corner st *(attach a st marker to center corner sc of each corner 3-sc group)*, work 23 sc across long edge, 3 sc in corner st, 6 sc evenly sp across ends of rows, 3 sc in corner st, 23 sc across long edge, 2 sc in same st as beg sc to complete last 3-sc corner group, join in beg sc. *(70 sc)*

Side

Rnd 6: Working in **back lps** *(see Stitch Guide)* for this rnd only, ch 2, hdc in each st around, moving st markers at each corner as rnd progresses, join in 2nd ch of beg ch-2.

Rnd 7: Sl st to 3rd st on short edge, **beg shell** *(see Special Stitches)* in same st, **fpdc** *(see Special Stitches)* around center corner hdc, sk next 2 sts, **shell** *(see Special Stitches)* in next st, [sk next 3 sts, shell in next st] 5 times, sk next 2 sts, fpdc around center corner hdc, sk 3 hdc, shell in next hdc on side edge, sk next 4 hdc, fpdc around center corner hdc, sk next 2 hdc, shell in next hdc, [sk next 3 sts, shell in next st] 5 times, sk next 2 sts, fpdc around center corner hdc, sl st to join in 3rd ch of beg ch-3. *(14 shells; 4 fpdc)*

Rnd 8: Sl st into ch-2 sp of shell, beg shell in same sp, fpdc around next fpdc, [shell in next ch-2 sp of next shell] 6 times, fpdc around next fpdc, shell in next shell, fpdc around next fpdc, [shell in next ch-2 sp of next shell] 6 times, fpdc around next fpdc, join in 3rd ch of beg ch-3.

Rnds 9–20: Rep rnd 8.

Note: The following row is worked across front and sides only, do not work across back.

Row 21 (RS): Now working in rows, ch 3 *(counts as first dc throughout)*, 3 dc in next ch-2 sp of next shell, dc in next fpdc, [3 dc in next ch-2 sp of next shell, dc in sp between shells] 5 times, [3 dc in next ch-2 sp of next shell, dc in next fpdc] twice, turn. *(33 dc)*

Row 22 (WS): Ch 1, sc in same dc as beg ch-1, sc in each of next 32 sts, fasten off. *(33 sc)*

Flap

Row 23 (RS): With back facing, attach delft with sl st in first sc of previous row, shell in ch-2 sp of each of next 6 shells across the back, sl st in last sc of previous row, turn. *(6 shells)*

Row 24: Sl st into ch-2 sp of shell, beg shell in same ch sp, shell in ch-2 sp of each of next 5 shells, turn.

Row 25: Rep row 24.

Row 26: Sl st into ch-2 sp of shell, ch 3, dc in same ch-2 sp, shell in each ch-2 sp of each of next 4 shells, 2 dc in last ch-2 sp of last shell, turn. *(4 shells; 2 dc each end)*

Row 27: Ch 3, shell in ch-2 sp of each of next 4 dc, dc in last dc of row, turn. *(4 shells; 1 dc each end)*

Row 28: Sl st into ch-2 sp of shell, ch 3, dc in same ch-2 sp, shell in each of next 2 shells, 2 dc in last ch-2 sp of last shell, turn. *(2 shells; 2 dc each end)*

Row 29: Ch 3, shell in ch-2 sp of each of next 2 shells, dc in last dc, turn. *(2 shells; 1 dc each end)*

Row 30: Sl st into ch-2 sp of shell, ch 3, dc in same ch-2 sp, ch 4 *(button lp)*, 2 dc in ch-2 sp of next shell, fasten off.

Edging

Row 31: With RS facing, working in ends of rows, attach delft with sc in first sc of row 22, work 20 sc evenly sp across edge to ch-4 button lp, work 4 sc over button lp, work 20 sc evenly sp across opposite ends of rows, ending with sc in last sc of row 22, turn. *(46 sc)*

Row 32: Ch 1, [sc in each of next 2 sc, **picot** *(see Special Stitches)*] across edge, fasten off.

Flower

Rnd 1: With true blue, ch 2, 6 sc in 2nd ch from hook. *(6 sc)*

Rnd 2: (Sl st, ch 2, 3 dc, ch 2, sl st) in each sc around, join in beg sl st, leaving a length of cotton, fasten off. *(6 petals)*

Leaf

With myrtle green, ch 8, sc in 2nd ch from hook, dc in next ch, tr in each of next 2 chs, dc in next ch, sc in next ch, sl st in next ch, *ch 7, sc in 2nd ch from hook, dc in next ch, tr in each of next 2 chs, dc in next ch, sc in next ch, sl st in same ch as last st, rep from * once, fasten off. Using photo as a guide, sew leaf group and flower centered over rnds 11 and 12 of front. Sew button centered over rnd 15.

Double-Deck Case

Base

Row 1: Rep row 1 of single-deck Case. *(25 hdc)*

Rows 2–8: Rep row 2 of single-deck Case. At the end of row 8, do not turn.

Rnd 9: Now working in rnds, ch 1, [work 11 sc across side edge of rows, 3 sc in corner *(attach a st marker to each center corner sc of each corner 3-sc group)*, work 23 sc across long edge, 3 sc in corner] twice, join in beg sc. *(80 sc)*

Side

Rnd 10: Working in back lps for this rnd only, ch 2, hdc in each st around, moving st markers at each corner, join in 2nd ch of beg ch-2.

Rnd 11: Sl st into next st, beg shell in same st, *[sk next 3 sts, shell in next st] twice, sk next 2 sts, fpdc around next st, sk next 2 sts, shell in next st, [sk next 3 sts, shell in next st] 5 times, sk next 2 sts, fpdc around next st**, sk next 2 sts, shell in next st, rep from * once, ending last rep at **, join in 3rd ch of beg ch-3. *(18 shells; 4 fpdc)*

Rnd 12: Sl st into ch-2 sp, beg shell in ch-2 sp of shell, shell in each of next 2 shells, fpdc around fpdc, shell in each of next 6 shells, fpdc around fpdc, shell in each of next 3 shells, fpdc around next fpdc, shell in each of next 6 shells, fpdc around fpdc, join in 3rd ch of beg ch-3.

Rnds 13–24: Rep rnd 12.

Row 25: Now working in rows, ch 3, 3 dc in next ch-2 sp of shell, [dc in sp between shells, 3 dc in next ch-2 sp of shell] twice, dc in next fpdc, [3 dc in next ch-2 sp of next shell, dc in sp between shells] 5 times, dc in fpdc, [3 dc in next ch-2 sp of next shell, dc in sp between shells] twice, 3 dc in next ch-2 sp of next shell, dc in next fpdc, turn. *(49 dc)*

Row 26: Ch 1, sc in same st as beg ch-11, sc in each of next 48 sc, fasten off. *(49 sc)*

Flap

Row 27: Rep row 23 of single-deck Case. *(6 shells)*

Rows 28–33: Rep row 24 of single-deck Case.

Row 34: Rep row 26 of single-deck

Case. *(4 shells; 2 dc each end)*

Rows 35–38: Rep rows 27–30 of Single-Deck Case.

Edging

Row 39: With RS facing and working in ends of rows, attach delft with sc in first sc of row 26, work 28 sc evenly sp in ends of rows to ch-4 button lp, work 4 sc over button lp, work 28 sc evenly sp across opposite edge of rows, sc in last sc of row 26, turn. *(62 sc)*

Row 40: Ch 1, [sc in each of next 2 sc, picot] across, fasten off.

Flower

Rnds 1 & 2: Rep rnds 1 and 2 of single-deck Case.

Leaf

Rep leaf of single-deck Case. Using photo as a guide, sew leaf group and flower centered on front over rnds 15 and 16. Sew button centered over rnd 20. ◆

Picnic Mats

DESIGN BY
KATHERINE ENG

Add a bright splash of tropical colors to a summer picnic with these festive, beaded table mats that are oh-so-quick and easy to stitch in fun, fabulous micro-fiber yarn.

Beginner •

Size

7¼ inches in diameter

Materials

- Lion Brand Micro Spun light (sport) weight yarn (2½ oz/168 yds/70g per skein):
    1½ oz each #194 lime, #148 turquoise and #186 mango
- Size E/4/3.5mm crochet hook or size needed to obtain gauge
- Size 10/1.15mm steel crochet hook
- Yarn needle
- ¼-inch faceted beads: 16 each lime, orange and blue

Gauge

Rnds 1 and 2 = 1¾ inches

Pattern Notes

Weave in loose ends as work progresses.

Join rounds with a slip stitch unless otherwise stated.

Size 10 steel hook is used only to thread beads onto sport weight yarn. Each yarn color makes one mat.

Mat

Make 3.

Rnd 1 (RS): With size E hook, ch 6, sl st to join in first ch to form a ring, ch 1, [sc in ring, ch 2] 8 times, in ring, join in beg sc. *(8 sc; 8 ch-2 sps)*

Rnd 2: Sl st into ch-2 sp, ch 1, [(sc, ch 2, sc) in ch-2 sp, ch 2] around, join in beg sc. *(16 sc)*

Rnd 3: Sl st into next ch-2 sp, ch 1, [(sc, ch 2, sc) in ch-2 sp, ch 3] around, join in beg sc. *(16 sc)*

Rnd 4: Sl st into ch-2 sp, ch 1, [(sc, ch 2, sc) in ch-2 sp, ch 1, sc in next ch-3 sp, ch 1] around, join in beg sc. *(24 sc)*

Rnd 5: Sl st into ch-2 sp, ch 1, [(sc, ch 2, sc) in ch-2 sp, ch 1, (sc, ch 2, sc) in next sc between ch-1 sps, ch 1] around, join in beg sc. *(32 sc)*

Rnds 6–8: Rep rnds 2–4. *(48 sc)*

Rnd 9: Sl st into ch-2 sp, ch 1, [(sc, ch 2, sc) in ch-2 sp, ch 6] 16 times, join in beg sc.

Rnd 10: Sl st into ch-2 sp, ch 1, [sc in ch-2 sp, (2 dc, ch 2, 2 dc) in next ch-5 sp] 16 times, fasten off.

Note: With size 10 steel crochet hook, thread 16 matching faceted beads onto sport weight yarn.

Rnd 11: With size E hook, attach yarn with a sl st in any sc between shells, *ch 3, sc in ch-2 sp, ch 1, pull bead down and forward, ch 2 over bead, sc in same ch-2 sp, ch 3, sl st in next sc, rep from * around, fasten off. ◆

Scrapbooking Keeper

DESIGN BY
CINDY CARLSON

Scrapbooking and crochet go hand-in-hand with this convenient holder that's great to take along on vacation for keeping photos and mementos organized in one easy place.

Beginner ●

Size
5 x 7½ inches

Materials
- J. & P. Coats size 3 fine (sport) weight yarn (100 yds per ball):
  1 ball each #126 Spanish red, #1 white and #486 navy
- Size C/2/2.75mm crochet hook or size needed to obtain gauge
- Yarn needle
- 1-inch wooden heart shape button

Gauge
10 hdc = 2 inches; 6 hdc rows = 2 inches

Pattern Notes
Weave in loose ends as work progresses.
Join rounds with a slip stitch unless otherwise stated.

Pocket
Note: Make 1 each Spanish red, white and navy.
Row 1: Beg at bottom of pocket, ch 37, sc in 2nd ch from hook, sc in each rem ch across, turn. *(36 sc)*
Row 2: Ch 2 *(counts as first hdc throughout)*, hdc in each st across, turn.
Rows 3–12: Rep row 2.
Row 13: Rep row 2, do not turn.
Note: On the Spanish red and white pockets only, work the following row.
Row 14: Working across top edge, ch 1, **reverse sc** *(see illustrations on page 92)* in each hdc across, fasten off.
Note: The following row is for the navy pocket only.
Row 14: Working across top edge, ch 1, sc in each hdc across, fasten off.

Flap
Row 1: With Spanish red, ch 17, sc in 2nd ch from hook, sc in each rem ch across, turn. *(16 sc)*
Row 2: Ch 1, sc in each sc across, fasten off, turn.
Row 3: Draw up a lp of white, ch 1, sc in each sc across, turn.
Row 4: Rep row 2.
Row 5: Draw up a lp of navy, ch 1, sc in each sc across, turn.

Row 6: Rep row 2.
Row 7: Draw up a lp of Spanish red, ch 1, sc in each sc across, turn.
Rows 8–36: Rep rows 2–7, ending last rep with row 6.

Button Loop
Attach white in side edge of flap between rows 18 and 19, ch 8, sl st in same st, fasten off.

Finishing
Place navy pocket on flat surface, place white pocket on top of navy and then Spanish red pocket on top of white pocket. Because of the sc row at top edge, navy pocket will be slightly larger at top edge.
Attach white in side edge of row 14 of navy section, ch 1, sc in same st as beg ch-1, ch 1, working through all thicknesses, [sc in side edge of pocket, ch 1] 14 times evenly sp down side edge to corner, work 3 sc in center corner, work 34 sc across opposite side of foundation ch, 3 sc in next corner, [ch 1, sc in side edge of pocket] 14 times up opposite side edge, ch 1, sc in navy section only in side edge of row 14, fasten off.
Thread yarn needle with a length of navy, holding side edge of flap

CONTINUED ON PAGE 109 ▶

Travel Neck Soother

DESIGN BY
CINDY CARLSON

Hot or cold, this soothing—and stylish!—neck roll helps take the aches and pains out of long, tiring trips. A handy fastening loop holds it securely in place even for vigorous sports activities.

Beginner •

Size
Fabric roll: 3½ x 18 inches
Crochet cover: 6½ x 34 inches

Materials
- Lily Sugar Babies light (light worsted) weight cotton yarn (5 oz/258 yds/140g per skein):
    1 skein #1215 baby aqua
- Size G/6/4mm crochet hook or size needed to obtain gauge
- Yarn needle
- Sewing machine
- Thread
- 1-inch floral shank buttons: 2
- Cotton print fabric: ⅓ yd
- 1¼ cup raw rice
- Scented essential oil
- Watersorb*: 3 teaspoons

*Watersorb can be found at www.watersorb.com or in garden stores. Ask for polymer-granules used for water retention for plants.

Gauge
3 shells and 4 dc = 4 inches; 6 shell rows = 4 inches
Check gauge to save time.

Pattern Notes
Weave in loose ends as work progresses.
Join rounds with a slip stitch unless otherwise stated.

Special Stitch
Shell: 5 dc in indicated st.

Fabric Roll
Make 2.
Cut 2 strips of printed fabric 4½ x 19 inches.
Fold first piece of fabric lengthwise with RS facing, allowing a ½-inch seam allowance; sew across one short edge and long edge, leaving rem short side open. Turn piece right side out and press. Sew second piece of fabric in same manner.
In first fabric roll, place 1¼ cups rice scented with essential oil. Turn raw edge to inside of fabric roll ½ inch and sew across open end twice. In the second fabric roll, place watersorb and sew opening closed in same manner.

Crochet Cover
Row 1: With baby aqua, ch 27, **shell** *(see Special Stitch)* in 6th ch from hook, sk next 2 chs, dc in next ch, [sk next 2 chs, shell in next ch, sk next 2 chs, dc in next ch] 3 times, turn. *(4 shells; 5 dc)*
Row 2: Ch 3 *(counts as first dc throughout)*, [shell in 3rd dc of next shell, dc in next single dc] 4 times, turn.
Rows 3–29: Rep row 2.
Row 30: Ch 1, sc in same st as beg ch-1, [ch 2, sk next 2 dc of shell, sc in next dc, sk next 2 dc of same shell, ch 2, sc in next dc] 4 times, do not turn. *(9 sc; 8 ch-2 sps)*
Row 31: Working in side edge of rows, ch 1, sc in side edge of row 30, 2 sc over side edge of each row, 3 sc in side edge of last row, fasten off.
Row 32: Working down opposite side edge of rows, attach baby aqua in side edge of row 1, ch 1, 3 sc in same sp, 2 sc in side edge of each row to last row, sc in last row, fasten off.

First End Tie
Row 1: Place crochet cover on a flat surface, fold each side edge of

CONTINUED ON PAGE 108 ▶

Kids' Carryalls

DESIGNS BY
MICHELE WILCOX

Intermediate • • •

Size
10½ x 11¼ inches, excluding handles

Materials
- Red Heart Classic medium (worsted) weight yarn (3½ oz/198 yds/99g per skein):
  - 8 oz #818 blue jewel
  - 1 oz each #111 eggshell and #1 white
  - ½ oz each #336 warm brown, #12 black, #746 cherry pink, #724 baby pink, #245 orange, #335 buff and #230 yellow
- Size H/8/5mm crochet hook or size needed to obtain gauge
- Yarn needle
- Fiberfill
- Stitch marker
- Black embroidery floss

These adorable, fun-to-stitch totes are sure to make trips to Grandma's house even more special for the kids. They're great for carrying snacks and games when traveling, too.

Bubble Bath Bear Bag

Gauge
9 sc = 2 inches; 9 sc rows = 2 inches

Pattern Notes
Weave in loose ends as work progresses.

Join rounds with a slip stitch unless otherwise stated.

When changing colors, drop first color to wrong side of work, pick up when needed. Fasten off each color when no longer needed.

Back
Row 1 (RS): With blue jewel, ch 46, sc in 2nd ch from hook, sc in each rem ch across, turn. *(45 sc)*

Rows 2–49: Ch 1, sc in each st across, turn.

Rnd 50: Now working in rnds around outer edge, ch 1, sc in each st and in end of each row around with 3 sc in each corner, join in beg sc, fasten off.

Front
Row 1: With buff, ch 46, sc in 2nd ch from hook, sc in each rem ch across, turn. *(45 sc)*

Rows 2–16: Ch 1, sc in each st across, turn. At the end of last rep,

fasten off.

Row 17: Attach blue jewel in first sc, ch 1, sc in each sc across, turn.

Row 18: Ch 1, sc in each of first 3 sts, **changing color** *(see Stitch Guide)* to baby pink in last st, sc in next st changing to blue jewel, [sc in each of next 3 sts changing to young rose in last st, sc in next st changing to blue jewel] 10 times, sc in last st, turn.

Row 19: Ch 1, sc in each st across, turn.

Rows 20–49: Rep rows 18 and 19 alternately.

Rnd 50: Now working in rnds, changing colors to match piece, ch 1, sc in each st and in end of each row around with 3 sc in each corner, join in beg sc, fasten off.

Rnd 51: Working in **front lps** *(see Stitch Guide)* for this rnd only, attach baby pink with a sc in any st, ch 3, sk next st, [sc in next st, ch 3, sk next st] around, join in beg sc, fasten off.

Handle
Make 2.

Row 1: With blue jewel, ch 6, sc in 2nd ch from hook, sc in each rem ch across, turn. *(5 sc)*

Rows 2–47: Ch 1, sc in each st across, turn.

Row 48: Ch 1, sc in each st across.

Rnd 49: Now working in rnds, sc in end of each row and in each st around with 3 sc in each corner, join in beg sc, fasten off.

Appliqués
Bear Head & Body

Row 1: Starting at bottom, with warm brown, ch 10, sc in 2nd ch from hook, sc in each rem ch across, turn. *(9 sc)*

Row 2: Ch 1, sc in each st across, turn.

Row 3: Rep row 2.

Row 4: Ch 1, **sc dec** *(see Stitch*

Guide) in next 2 sc, sc in each st across to last 2 sts, sc dec in next 2 sts, turn. *(7 sc)*

Row 5: Rep row 2.

Rows 6 & 7: Rep row 4. *(3 sc)*

Rows 8–10: Ch 1, 2 sc in first st, sc in each st across to last st, 2 sc in last st, turn. *(9 sc)*

Rows 11–13: Rep row 2.

Row 14: Rep row 4. *(7 sc)*

Row 15: Rep row 4, do not turn. *(5 sc)*

Rnd 16: Now working in rnds around outer edge, ch 1, sc in end of each row and in each st around with 3 sc in each bottom corner, join in beg sc, fasten off.

Ear

Make 2.

Row 1: With warm brown, ch 2, 6 sc in second ch from hook, turn. *(6 sc)*

Row 2: Ch 1, 2 sc in each st across, fasten off. *(12 sc)*

Arm

Row 1: With warm brown, ch 4, sc in 2nd ch from hook, sc in each of next 2 ch, turn. *(3 sc)*

Rows 2–12: Ch 1, sc in each st across, turn.

Row 13: Ch 1, [insert hook in next st, yo, draw up a lp] 3 times, yo, draw through all 4 lps on hook, fasten off.

Muzzle

Rnd 1: With buff, ch 2, 6 sc in 2nd ch from hook, do not join. *(6 sc)*

Rnd 2: [Sc in next st, 2 sc in next st] 3 times, sl st in next st, fasten off. *(9 sc)*

Sew muzzle to bear head over rnds 9–12.

With black embroidery floss, working in **satin stitch** *(see illustration)*, embroider eyes ¾ inch apart on rnd 12 at each side of muzzle. Using bear facial illustration as a guide, embroider nose over rnd 1 of muzzle and working with **straight stitches** *(see*

illustration), embroider mouth over rnds 1 and 2.

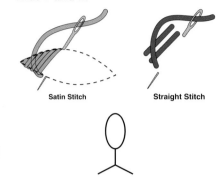

Satin Stitch   Straight Stitch

Bear Facial Illustration

Brush

With cherry pink, ch 12, sc in 2nd ch from hook, sc in each of next 2 chs, sl st in each of next 4 chs, dc in each of next 3 chs, sc in last ch, fasten off. *(11 sts)*

Duck

Row 1: With yellow, ch 6, sc in 2nd ch from hook, sc in each ch across, turn. *(5 sc)*

Row 2: Ch 1, 2 sc in first sc, sc in each st across with 2 sc in last st, turn. *(7 sc)*

Row 3: Ch 1, sc in each st across, turn.

Row 4: Ch 1, sc dec in next 2 sts, sc in next st leaving last 4 sts unworked, turn. *(2 sc)*

Row 5: Ch 1, 2 sc in each st across, turn. *(4 sc)*

Row 6: Ch 1, [insert hook in next sc, yo, draw up a lp] 4 times, yo, draw through all 5 lps on hook, fasten off. Using photo as a guide, with black embroidery floss, embroider a **French knot** *(see illustration)* eye on row 5.

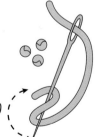

French Knot

Tub

Row 1: With eggshell, ch 20, sc in 2nd ch from hook, sc in each rem ch across, turn. *(19 sc)*

Row 2: Ch 1, 2 sc in first st, sc in each st across, ending with 2 sc in

last st, turn. *(21 sc)*

Row 3: Ch 1, sc in each st across, turn.

Rows 4–7: Rep rows 2 and 3. *(25 sc)*

Rows 8–12: Rep row 3.

Row 13: Ch 1, 2 sc in first st, [sc in next st, 2 sc in next st] across, do not turn. *(38 sc)*

Rnd 14: Now working in rnds around outer edge, ch 1, sc in end of each row and in each st around, join in beg sc, fasten off.

Tub Leg

Make 2

Note: *Work in continuous rnds; do not join or turn unless otherwise stated. Mark first st of each rnd.*

Rnd 1: With eggshell, ch 2, 6 sc in 2nd ch from hook. *(6 sc)*

Rnds 2 & 3: Sc in each st around.

Rnd 4: [Sc in next st, 2 sc in next st] 3 times. *(9 sc)*

Rnds 5 & 6: Sc in each st around. At the end of rnd 6, leaving a length of yarn, fasten off. Sew opening closed.

Large Bubbles

With white bulky yarn, [ch 4, 5 dc in 4th ch from hook, drop lp from hook, insert hook in top ch of ch-4, pick up dropped lp and draw through st on hook] 39 times, fasten off.

Small Bubbles

With white bulky yarn, [ch 3, 3 hdc in 3rd ch from hook, drop lp from hook, insert hook in top of ch-3, pick up dropped lp and draw through st on hook] 10 times, fasten off.

Finishing

Fold rnds 11–14 of tub to outside, sew tub centered on front over rnds 11–26.

Insert rows 1 and 2 of bear head & body inside tub, sew to front, stuffing head lightly with fiberfill. Using photo as a guide, sew rem appliqué pieces onto front.

With orange, using **lazy-daisy stitch** *(see illustration)*, embroider duck's beak to head. Using straight stitches, embroider bristles on brush.

Lazy-Daisy Stitch

Assembly

Hold front and back WS tog, matching sts, working in back lps only, sew sides and bottom tog leaving top unsewn.

Working through all thicknesses, sew each end of one handle 2 inches apart to top edge on front. Rep with 2nd handle on back.

Kitten in a Basket

Intermediate ●●●

Size

12½ x 13½ inches, excluding handles

Materials

- Red Heart Classic medium (worsted) weight yarn (3½ oz/198 yds/99g per skein):
    8 oz #355 light teal
    2½ oz #645 honey gold
    ½ oz each #508 peacock green, #719 lily pink and #730 grenadine
- 1½ oz fuzzy white bulky (chunky) bulky weight yarn
- Sizes F/5/3.75mm and H/8/5mm crochet hooks or sizes needed to obtain gauge
- Tapestry needle
- Sewing needle
- 1 skein black embroidery floss
- 1-inch-wide ribbon: 16 inches
- Jingle bell
- Stitch marker

Gauge

Size F hook: 9 dc = 2 inches; 2 shells, 1 sc = 2½ inches; 7 shell rows = 3 inches
Size H hook: 7 sc = 2 inches; 4 sc rows = 1 inch

Pattern Notes

Weave in loose ends as work progresses.
Join rounds with a slip stitch unless otherwise stated.
Use size F hook unless otherwise stated.

Special Stitches

Shell: 5 dc in indicated st.
Front post double crochet (fpdc): Yo, insert hook front to back to front again around vertical post of indicated st, yo, draw up a lp, [yo, draw through 2 lps on hook] twice.

Back post double crochet (bpdc): Yo, insert hook back to front to back again around vertical post of indicated st, yo, draw up a lp, [yo, draw through 2 lps on hook] twice.

Side

Make 2.
Row 1: With light teal, ch 56, sc in 2nd ch from hook, [sk next 2 chs, **shell** *(see Special Stitches)* in next ch, sk next 2 chs, sc in next ch] across, turn. *(9 shells)*
Row 2: Ch 3 *(counts as first dc throughout)*, 2 dc in same st, sc in center dc of next shell, [shell in next sc, sc in center dc of next shell] 8 times, 3 dc in last sc, turn. *(9 sc; 8 shells; 6 dc)*
Row 3: Ch 1, sc in first st, sk next 2 sts, shell in next sc, [sc in center dc of next shell, shell in next sc] 8 times, sk

CONTINUED ON PAGE 110 ▶

83

Jazzy Gems

DESIGN BY
WHITNEY CHRISTMAS

A large-size hook, super-bulky yarn and our Easy Tunisian™ crochet technique make this chic, colorful tote a fun, quick project that's perfect for a campus carryall or travel bag.

Intermediate ● ● ●

Size

12 x 12 inches x 4 inches deep and 30-inch straps

Materials

- Lion Brand Jiffy Thick & Quick super bulky (super chunky) weight yarn (5 oz/84 yds/140g per skein): 4 skeins #207 green mountains
- Lion Brand Fun Fur bulky (chunky) weight eyelash novelty yarn (1¾ oz/60 yds/50g per skein): 30 yds #109 sapphire
- Size J/10/6mm crochet hook
- Sizes N/13/9mm and P/15/10mm Easy Tunisian™ crochet hooks or sizes needed to obtain gauge
- Tapestry needle

Gauge

Size P Tunisian hook and super-bulky yarn: 2 sts = 1 inch; 5 rows = 3 inches

Pattern Notes

Weave in loose ends as work progresses.
Join rounds with a slip stitch unless otherwise stated.

Special Stitches

Tunisian simple stitch (tss): Insert hook under vertical thread, yo, draw up a lp.

Tunisian knit stitch (tks): Inserting the hook through center of the st to back of the piece, yo, draw up a lp.

Tunisian purl stitch (tps): Insert hook from back to front under the vertical thread, yo, draw up a lp.

Return: Yo, draw through first lp on hook, [yo, draw through 2 lps on hook] across until 1 lp remains on hook.

Bag

Make 2.

Row 1: With size N hook and green mountains, ch 31, with size P hook, insert hook in 2nd ch from hook, yo, draw up a lp, [insert hook in next ch, yo, draw up a lp] across *(31 lps on hook)*, yo, draw through first lp on hook, [yo, draw through 2 lps on hook] across until 1 lp remains on hook *(return completed)*.

Row 2: Work **tss** *(see Special Stitches)* across row, return.

Row 3: Rep row 2.

Row 4: Work **tps** *(see Special Stitches)* across row, return.

Rows 5–13: Work **tks** *(see Special Stitches)* across row, return.

Row 14: Rep row 4.

Rows 15–25: Rep row 2.

Row 26: Sk first vertical bar and sl st in each of next 3 vertical bars, pick up lps as to tps in each of next 25 sts, work 1 tss, sl st in each of next 2 sts, leaving a 20-inch length of yarn for sewing, fasten off. *(25 lps on hook)* To work lps off, join yarn in first lp and work off as for tps.

Rows 27–30: Rep row 2.

Row 31: With size N hook, sk first vertical bar, [insert hook under next vertical bar, yo, draw through 2 lps on hook] across, leaving a long length of yarn, fasten off.

Strap

Make 2.

Row 1: With green mountains yarn

CONTINUED ON PAGE 111 ▶

Bee Tidy

DESIGN BY
SUE PENROD

This whimsical little fellow will help kids tidy up their room by providing a quick, easy place to hang up their jackets. He works up quick-as-a-wink in medium weight yarn.

Beginner •

Size
4 x 5 inches

Materials
- Red Heart Super Saver medium (worsted) weight yarn (3 oz/170 yds/85g per skein):
  - ½ oz #312 black
  - 40 yds each #324 bright yellow and #245 orange
  - 1 yd each #390 cherry red and #311 white
- Size G/6/4mm crochet hook or size needed to obtain gauge
- Yarn needle
- Stitch marker
- 3-inch plastic peel and stick wall hook
- Craft glue
- Scrap of fiberfill

Gauge
4 sc = 1 inch; 4 sc rows = 1 inch

Pattern Notes
Weave in loose ends as work progresses.
Join rounds with a slip stitch unless otherwise stated.

Body
Rnd 1: Starting at bottom of body, with black, ch 4, join in first ch to form a ring, ch 1, 2 sc in each ch around, do not join, place a marker. *(8 sc)*
Rnd 2: Ch 1, sc in each sc around.
Rnds 3–12: Rep rnd 2.
Rnd 13: Sc in next sc, ch 4, sk each of next 4 sc, sc in each of next 3 sc. *(4 sc; ch-4 sp)*
Rnd 14: 2 sc in next sc, 2 sc in each of next 4 chs, 2 sc in each of next 3 sc. *(16 sc)*
Rnds 15–20: Rep rnd 2.
Rnd 21: Sc in every other sc. *(8 sc)*

Head
Rnd 22: 2 sc in each of next 8 sc. *(16 sc)*
Rnds 23–25: Rep rnd 2.
Stuff head lightly with fiberfill.
Rnd 26: Rep rnd 21. *(8 sc)*
Rnd 27: Sl in every other sc, fasten off. *(4 sl sts)*

Feelers
Cut a 4-inch length of black yarn.

Fold strand in half, insert hook in center top of head, draw strand through at fold to form a lp on hook, draw cut ends through lp on hook. Tie an overhand knot 1 inch from head on each end, trim ends beyond each knot.

Left Side Upper Wing
Row 1: Working in side edge of body, attach bright yellow in sp between rnds 19 and 20 with a sl st, ch 8, sc in 2nd ch from hook, sc in each of next 6 chs, sl st in same st between rnd 19 and 20, turn. *(7 sc)*
Row 2: Sk first sc, sc in each rem sc across, turn. *(6 sc)*
Row 3: Ch 1, sc in each of next 6 sc, sl st in next st of body between rnds 20 and 21, turn. *(6 sc)*
Row 4: Rep row 2. *(5 sc)*
Row 5: Ch 1, sc in each of next 5 sc, sl st in same st of body between rnds 20 and 21, fasten off. *(5 sc)*

Left Side Lower Wing
Row 1: Working in side edge of body below upper wing, attach orange between rnds 17 and 18, ch 5, sc in 2nd ch from hook, sc in each of next 3 chs, sl st in same st between rnds 17 and 18, turn. *(4 sc)*
Row 2: Sc in each sc across,

turn. *(4 sc)*

Row 3: Ch 1, sc in each sc across, sl st in sp between rnd 18 and 19, turn. *(4 sc)*

Row 4: Ch 1, sc dec in next 2 sc, sc in each of next 2 sc, fasten off. *(3 sc)*

Right Side Lower Wing

Row 1: Working in side edge of body opposite left side lower wing, attach orange between rnds 18 and 19, ch 4, sc in 2nd ch from hook, sc in each of next 2 chs, sl st in same st between rnds 18 and 19, turn. *(3 sc)*

Row 2: Ch 1, 2 sc in first sc, sc in each of next 2 sc, turn. *(4 sc)*

Row 3: Ch 1, sc in each of next 4 sc, sl st in sp between rnds 17 and 18, turn.

Row 4: Ch 1, sc in each of next 4 sc, fasten off.

Right Side Upper Wing

Row 1: Working in side edge of body above lower wing opposite left side upper wing, attach bright yellow in sp between rnds 20 and 21, ch 6, sc in 2nd ch from hook, sc in each rem ch across, sl st in same sp between rnds 20 and 21, turn. *(5 sc)*

Row 2: Sc in each sc across, turn.

Row 3: Ch 1, 2 sc in first sc, sc in each rem sc across, sl st in sp between rnds 19 and 20, turn. *(6 sc)*

Row 4: Rep row 2.

Row 5: Ch 1, 2 sc in first sc, sc in each rem sc, sl st in same sp between rnds 19 and 20, fasten off. *(7 sc)*

Wing trim

Make 4.

Row 1: Attach black in side edge of wing next to body, ch 1, sc evenly sp around outer edge of wing, working 2 sc in each outer corner and ending wing trim at side edge of wing next to body, fasten off.

Finishing

Embroider eyes with a white **French knot** *(see illustration)* and

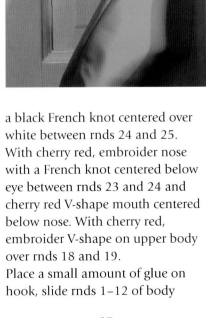

a black French knot centered over white between rnds 24 and 25. With cherry red, embroider nose with a French knot centered below eye between rnds 23 and 24 and cherry red V-shape mouth centered below nose. With cherry red, embroider V-shape on upper body over rnds 18 and 19.

Place a small amount of glue on hook, slide rnds 1–12 of body

over hook. Place a small amount of glue on flat portion of 3-inch plastic hook and press body to plastic to secure body to piece. Shape each wing and allow glue to dry. ◆

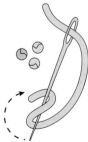

French Knot

Say it With Flowers

DESIGNS BY
NANCY NEHRING

The personal touch of a hand-written note never goes out of style, and these beautiful cards accented with beaded crochet flowers are sure to be appreciated by all who receive them.

Intermediate •••

Size
Primrose: 2 x 6¾ inches
Clematis: 2¼ x 6¼ inches
Rose: 4½ x 4½ inches
Forget-Me-Not: 2½ x 6½ inches

Materials
- Crochet cotton size 10 (350 yds per ball):
    50 yds each shaded purples, green, pale yellow, dark ecru, pink, dark green, white and blue
    5 yds yellow
- Size 7/1.65mm steel crochet hook or size needed to obtain gauge
- Tapestry needle
- ⅛-inch paper punch
- Various color 6mm beads: 4
- Glue stick
- White glue
- 5⅛ x 7-inch blank cards: 1 each of lavender, cream, pink and white
- 3½ x 7-inch cream decorative paper
- Straight pins
- Spray starch

Gauge
8 sts = 1 inch

Pattern Notes
Weave in loose ends as work progresses.
Join rounds with a slip stitch unless otherwise stated.

Special Stitch
Petal: Ch 4, *yo hook twice, insert hook in ring, yo, draw up a lp, [yo, draw through 2 lps on hook] twice, yo, draw through all 3 lps on hook, ch 4, sc in ring.

Primrose

Card Preparation
Working with lavender card, cut 1¾ inches from long edge of front of card. Punch 6 evenly spaced holes across card front, ⅛-inch from cut edge.

Flowers
Row 1: With shaded purples, ch 8, sl st in first ch to form a ring, [work 5 **petals** *(see Special Stitch)* in ring, ch 20, sl st in 8th ch from hook to form a ring] 4 times, 5 petals in ring, sl st in first ch of first petal of this flower, fasten off. *(5 flowers)*

Edging
Row 2: Attach green in last st of row 1, ch 10, sl st in tip of first petal of last flower, fasten off, turn, with WS facing, attach green to first sl st of row 1, ch 10, sl st in tip of last petal of first flower, turn, ch 1, 5 sc over green lp, sc in first hole of card, 8 sc over remainder of green ch, [8 sc over purple lp, sc in next hole of card, 8 sc over remainder of same ch lp] 4 times, 8 sc over next green lp, sc in last hole of card, 5 sc over remainder of green lp, fasten off. Open card and lightly steam flowers only to fit size of card.

Clematis

Flowers
Row 1: With pale yellow, [ch 16, sc in 3rd ch from hook, dc in next ch, tr in each of next 3 chs, dc in next ch, sc in next ch, ch 9, sc in 3rd ch from hook, dc in next ch, tr in each of next 3 chs, dc in next ch, sc in next ch] 4 times, ch 9, sc in 3rd ch from hook, dc in next ch, tr in each of next 3 chs, dc in next ch, sc in next ch, working back along other side of chs, *[ch 9, sc in 3rd ch from hook, dc in next ch, tr in each of

CONTINUED ON PAGE 112 ▶

Watermelon Backpack

DESIGN BY
ANN SMITH

Crochet this cute, colorful carryall to pack a picnic lunch for a fun trip to the zoo. It works up easily in double strands of size 3 cotton thread in delicious watermelon colors!

Intermediate •••

Size
Approximately 8 inches tall x
  6 inches deep x 11 inches wide

Materials
• J. & P. Coats Speed-Cro-Sheen fine (sport) weight crochet cotton (100 yds per ball):
    8 balls #12 black
    4 balls #1 white
    2 balls each #46A mid rose and #48 hunter green
• Size E/4/3.5mm crochet hook or size needed to obtain gauge
• Yarn needle
• ¾-inch black button
• ½-inch black buttons: 5
• 10¾ x 5-inch plastic canvas or cardboard
• Stitch markers

Gauge
With 2 strands of crochet cotton held tog, 15 sc = 4 inches; 15 sc rows = 4 inches

Pattern Notes
Weave in loose ends as work progresses.
Join rounds with a slip stitch unless otherwise stated.
Work with 2 strands of crochet cotton held tog throughout unless otherwise stated.

Base
Rnd 1: With 2 strands of black, ch 25, 3 sc in 2nd ch from hook, sc in each of next 22 chs, 3 sc in last ch, working on opposite side of foundation ch, sc in each of next 22 chs, join in beg sc. *(50 sc)*

Rnd 2: Ch 1, 3 sc in same sc as beg ch-1, *sc in next sc, 3 sc in next sc, sc in each of next 22 sc**, 3 sc in next sc, rep from * to **, join in beg sc. *(58 sc)*

Rnd 3: Ch 1, sc in same sc as beg ch-1, *3 sc in next sc, sc in each of next 3 sc, 3 sc in next sc**, sc in each of next 24 sc, rep from * to **, sc in each of next 23 sc, join in beg sc. *(66 sc)*

Rnd 4: Ch 1, sc in same sc as beg ch-1, sc in next sc, *3 sc in next sc, sc in each of next 5 sc, 3 sc in next sc**, sc in each of next 26 sc, rep from * to **, sc in each of next 24 sc, join in beg sc. *(74 sc)*

Rnd 5: Ch 1, sc in same sc as beg ch-1, sc in each of next 2 sc, *3 sc in next sc, sc in each of next 7 sc, 33 sc in next sc**, sc in each of next 28 sc, rep from * to **, sc in each of next 25 sc, join in beg sc. *(82 sc)*

Rnd 6: Ch 1, sc in same sc as beg ch-1, sc in each of next 3 sc, *3 sc in next sc, sc in each of next 9 sc, 3 sc in next sc**, sc in each of next 30 sc, rep from * to **, sc in each of next 26 sc, join in beg sc. *(90 sc)*

Rnd 7: Ch 1, sc in same sc as beg ch-1, sc in each of next 4 sc, *3 sc in next sc, sc in each of next 11 sc, 3 sc in next sc**, sc in each of next 32 sc, rep from * to **, sc in each of next 27 sc, join in beg sc. *(98 sc)*

Rnd 8: Ch 1, sc in same sc as beg ch-1, sc in each of next 5 sc, *3 sc in next sc, sc in each of next 13 sc, 3 sc in next sc**, sc in each of next 34 sc, rep from * to **, sc in each of next 28 sc, join in beg sc, fasten off. *(106 sc)*

Base should measure 11 x 14½ inches.

Body

Rnd 1: With RS facing, attach 2 strands of black with a sl st in center st of one long side, ch 1, sc in same sc as joining, sc in each sc around, join in beg sc, **change color** (*see Stitch Guide*) to white. (*106 sc*)

Rnd 2: Ch 1, sc in each sc around, join in beg sc, change to black.

Rnd 3: Ch 1, sc in each sc around, join in beg sc, change to white.

Rnds 4–8: Work in established stripe pattern.

Rnd 9: Ch 1, sc in each of first 16 sc, *sc dec (*see Stitch Guide*) in next 2 sc, sc in next sc, sc dec in next 2 sc**, sc in each of next 11 sc, rep from * to **, sc in each of next 32 sc, rep from * to **, sc in each of next 11 sc, rep from * to **, sc in each of next 16 sc, join in beg sc, change to white. (*98 sc*)

Rnds 10–18: Work in established stripe pattern.

Rnd 19: Ch 1, sc in each of first 15 sc, *sc dec in next 2 sc, sc in next sc, sc dec in next 2 sc**, sc in each of next 9 sc, rep from * to **, sc in each of next 30 sc, rep from * to **, sc in each of next 9 sc, rep from * to **, sc in each of next 15 sc, join in beg sc, change to white. (*90 sc*)

Rnds 20–30: Work in established stripe pattern. At end of last rep, fasten off white.

Rnd 31: Ch 1, sc in same sc as beg ch-1, ch 1, sk 1 sc, [sc in next sc, ch 1, sk 1 sc] around, join in beg sc.

Rnd 32: Ch 1, sc in each sc and each ch-1 sp around, join in beg sc, fasten off.

Drawstring

Using 2 strands of hunter green, ch 150, fasten off. Beg at seam, weave drawstring through eyelet formed on rnd 31. Tie each end with an overhand knot.

Pocket

Row 1 (RS): Using 2 strands of black, ch 21, sc in 2nd ch from hook, sc in each rem ch across, drop black. (*20 sc*)

Row 2: With RS facing, attach 2 strands of white in first sc of previous row with a sl st, ch 1, sc in same sc as beg ch-1, sc in each sc across, draw lp of 2 strands of black through white, turn.

Row 3: Ch 1, sc in each sc across, drop black.

Row 4: With white, ch 1, sc in each sc across, draw lp of 2 strands of black through white, turn.

Rows 5–24: [Rep rows 3 and 4] 10 times. At the end of last rep, fasten off both colors.

Pocket edging

Row 1: With RS facing, attach 2 strands of black at corner on one side edge with a sl st, ch 1, work 21 sc evenly sp along side, 3 sc in corner, 20 sc across edge, 3 sc in corner, 21 sc evenly sp along second side, turn.

Row 2: Ch 1, sc in each sc of row 1, turn.

Row 3: Ch 1, working in back lps only, sc in each st of row 2, turn.

Rows 4–9: Rep rows 2 and 3 alternately, fasten off.

Beg at base, place markers 3 inches from the side edge of the center front. Run a basting line to mark for a 6-inch square pocket, removing markers as you sew. Position pocket along basting lines and whipstitch in place to form accordion edges. Sew ¾-inch button onto center of top white stripe.

Flap

Pull up on drawstring so a small inset fold forms at each edge and pocket is at center front. Turn bag so back is facing and mark center 28 sts of rnd 30.

Row 1: Attach 2 strands of pink with a sl st to first marked sc in rnd 30 (*before eyelets*), ch 1, *insert hook from front to back to front again around post of sc, complete sc, rep from * around post of next 27 marked sc, turn. (*28 sc*)

Row 2: Ch 1, sc in each sc across, turn.

Rep row 2 until flap measures 4½ inches from beg.

Dec row: Ch 1, sc dec in next 2 sc, sc in each sc across to last 2 sc, sc dec in next 2 sc, turn. (*26 sc*)

Rep dec row until 20 sts rem, fasten off.

Edging

Row 1: With RS facing, attach 2 strands of white in side of row 1 of flap, ch 1, work 21 sc evenly sp along side, 20 sc along edge, 21 sc evenly sp along side, turn.

Row 2: Ch 1, sc in each sc across, fasten off.

Row 3: With RS facing, attach 2 strands of hunter green, ch 1, sc in each sc across, turn.

Row 4: Ch 1, sc in each of next 30 sc, ch 2, sk next 2 sc, sc in each of next 30 sc, turn.

Row 5: Ch 1, sc in each sc across, working 2 sc in ch-2 sp, turn.

Row 6: Ch 1, **reverse sc** (*see illustration*) across, fasten off. Using photo as a guide, sew ½-inch black buttons to flap; fold flap over pocket.

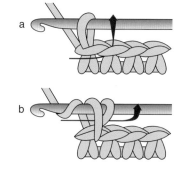

Reverse Single Crochet

Handle

With pocket side facing, attach 2 strands of black over same sc post as 10th st from right edge, ch 19, sk 8 sc, sl st over same black sc post as 10th pink sc from opposite edge,

CONTINUED ON PAGE 111 ▶

Crochet Time

This uniquely styled clock will constantly remind you that it's always time to crochet! Each "number" features a different pattern that will help you increase your stitching skills.

DESIGN BY
BELINDA "BENDY" CARTER

Intermediate •••

Size
12 inches in diameter

Materials
- South Maid size 10 crochet cotton (350 yds per ball):
  - 2 balls #1 white
  - 50 yds #12 black
  - 25 yds each #494 victory red, #487 dark royal, #143 soft yellow, #484 myrtle, #458 purple, #434 cappuccino, #497 burgundy, #480 delft, #421 goldenrod, #449 forest green, #495 wood violet and #433 camel
- Sizes 7/1.65mm, 3/2.10mm and 00/2.70mm steel crochet hooks or sizes needed to obtain gauge
- Steel crochet hook size desired to attach as embellishment to clock
- Tapestry needle
- Beading needle
- Stitch marker
- Rocaille beads
  - red: 52
  - ice blue: 84
- Clear-drying tacky glue
- $^{15}/_{16}$ x $11^{7}/_{8}$-inch plastic foam disk
- $^{13}/_{16}$ x $11^{7}/_{8}$-inch plastic foam wreath
- Battery operated clock to fit ¾-inch clock face with two 2½-inch black clock hands
- Mounting hardware
- Hanger

Gauge
Size 00 hook: 5 rnds = 1 inch

Size 3 hook: Ch 26 = 3 inches
Size 7 hook: One square = 1½ inches
Check gauge to save time.

Pattern Notes
Weave in loose ends as work progresses.
Do not join rounds unless otherwise stated. Use stitch marker to mark rounds.

Special Stitches
Puff stitch (puff st): [Yo, insert hook in indicated st, yo, draw up a lp] 3 times, yo, draw through all 7 lps on hook.

Bullion stitch (bullion st): Yo 5 times, insert hook in indicated st, yo, draw up a lp, yo, draw through all 7 lps on hook.

Front post double triple treble crochet (fpdtrtr): Yo hook 5 times, insert hook front to back to front again around indicated st, yo, draw up a lp, [yo, draw through 2 lps on hook] 6 times.

Front post triple treble crochet (fptrtr): Yo hook 4 times, insert hook front to back to front again around vertical post of indicated st, yo, draw up a lp, [yo, draw through 2 lps on hook] 5 times.

Back post triple treble crochet (bptrtr): Yo hook 4 times, insert hook back to front to back again around vertical post of indicated st, yo, draw up a lp, [yo, draw through 2 lps on hook] 5 times.

Back post double treble crochet (bpdtr): Yo hook 3 times, insert hook back to front to back again around vertical post of indicated st, yo, draw up a lp, [yo, draw through 2 lps on hook] 4 times.

Clock Face Cover
Rnd 1 (RS): With size 00 hook and 2 strands of white held tog, ch 6, sl st to join in first ch to form a ring, ch 1, 12 sc in ring, do not join rnds, use st marker to mark rnds. *(12 sc)*
Rnd 2: [2 sc in next st, sc in next st] 6 times. *(18 sc)*
Rnd 3: [2 sc in next sc, sc in each of next 2 sc] 6 times. *(24 sc)*
Rnd 4: [2 sc in next sc, sc in each of next 3 sc] 6 times. *(30 sc)*
Rnds 5–27: Inc 6 sc evenly sp around each rnd and add 1 sc between each inc on each rnd. *(168 sc)*
Rnd 28: [2 sc in next sc, sc in each of next 27 sc] 6 times. *(174 sc)*
Rnds 29–34: Sc in each sc around. At the end of rnd 34, sl st in next st, fasten off.

Clock Works
Make a hole in center of plastic foam disk big enough for clock shaft to go through. Aligning center of clock cover with hole in disk, glue cover on disk, completely covering top and sides of disk. Insert shaft in hole from behind, pressing hard enough to form indentation of clock works on back of disk and then remove. Using scissors, scrape approximately ¼ inch plastic foam off back of disk where indentation was made so that clock fits slightly inside disk and clock hands can be attached to front of clock. Attach clock hands according to package directions.

Clock Border
Rnd 1: With size 00 hook and 2 strands of white held tog, ch 150, using care not to twist ch, sl st in first ch to form a ring, ch 1, [2 sc in next ch, sc in each of next 24 chs] 6 times, do not join rnds, use a st marker. *(156 sc)*
Rnd 2: [2 sc in next sc, sc in each of next 25 sc] 6 times. *(162 sc)*
Rnd 3: [2 sc in next sc, sc in each of next 26 sc] 6 times. *(168 sc)*
Rnd 4: [2 sc in next sc, sc in each of next 27 sc] 6 times. *(174 sc)*
Rnd 5: Sc in each sc around.
Rnds 6–11: Rep rnd 5.
Rnd 12: [Sc dec *(see Stitch Guide)* in next 2 sc, sc in each of next 27 sc] 6 times. *(168 sc)*
Rnd 13: [Sc dec in next 2 sc, sc in each of next 26 sc] 6 times. *(162 sc)*
Rnd 14: [Sc dec in next 2 sc, sc in each of next 25 sc] 6 times. *(156 sc)*
Rnd 15: [Sc dec in next 2 sc, sc in each of next 24 sc] 6 times. *(150 sc)*
Rnd 16: [Sc dec in next 2 sc, sc in each of next 23 sc] 6 times. *(144 sc)*
Rnd 17: [Sc dec in next 2 sc, sc in each of next 22 sc] 6 times. *(138 sc)*
Rnds 18–24: Rep rnd 5.
Rnd 25: [2 sc in next sc, sc in each of next 22 sc] 6 times. *(144 sc)*
Rnd 26: [2 sc in next sc, sc in each of next 23 sc] 6 times, leaving a long length of cotton, fasten off. *(150 sc)*
Wrap clock border around plastic foam disk so that rnds 1 and 26 come tog at back of ring. Sew rnd 26 to opposite side of foundation ch of rnd 1. Glue ring to front of disk.

Clock Squares
Note: For all clock squares, use size 7 steel hook and 1 strand of cotton.

One O'clock
Row 1: Thread 52 red beads onto victory red cotton. With size 7 hook, ch 17, sc in 2nd ch from hook, [ch 2, push up 4 beads, ch 1 over beads, ch 2, sk next 4 chs, sc in next ch] 3 times, turn.
Row 2: Ch 5 *(counts as first dc, ch-2 throughout)*, sc between 2nd and 3rd bead of previous row, [ch 2, push up 4 beads, ch 1 over beads, ch 2, sc between 2nd and 3rd beads of previous row] twice, ch 2, dc in last st, turn.
Row 3: Ch 5, push up 4 beads, ch 1 over beads, ch 2, [sc between 2nd and 3rd beads of previous row, ch 2, push up 4 beads, ch 1 over beads, ch 2] twice, dc in 3rd ch of last ch-5 sp, turn.
Rows 4 & 5: Rep rows 2 and 3.
Row 6: Ch 5, sc between 2nd and 3rd beads, [ch 4, sc between 2nd and 3rd beads] twice, ch 2, dc in last st, fasten off.

Two O'clock

Row 1: With dark royal, ch 18, dc in 4th ch from hook, dc in each of next 2 chs, [ch 2, sk next 2 chs, dc in each of next 4 chs] twice, turn.

Row 2: Ch 5 (counts as first dc, ch 2), [sk next 2 dc, dc in next dc, 2 dc in ch-2 sp, dc in next dc, ch 2] twice, sk next 2 dc, dc in last dc, turn.

Row 3: Ch 3 (counts as first dc), 2 dc in ch-2 sp, [dc in next dc, ch 2, sk next 2 dc, dc in next dc, 2 dc in ch-2 sp] twice, dc in last dc, turn. Rep rows 2 and 3 until piece measures 1½ inches, fasten off.

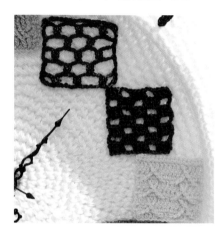

Three O'clock

Row 1: With soft yellow, ch 19, dc in 4th ch from hook, dc in each rem ch across, turn. (17 dc)

Row 2: Ch 3, dc in each st across, turn.

Row 3: Ch 3, dc in each of next 2 dc, [fpdtrtr (see Special Stitches) 2 rows below and 4 sts to the left, dc in next 2 dc, fpdtrtr 2 rows below and 4 sts to the right, dc in each of next 3 dc] twice, turn. (17 sts)

Rows 4–7: Rep rows 2 and 3.

Row 8: Ch 1, sc in each st across, fasten off.

Four O'clock

Row 1: With myrtle green, ch 20, dc in 6th ch from hook, [ch 1, sk next ch, puff st (see Special Stitches) in next ch, ch 1, sk next ch, dc in next ch] 3 times, ch 1, sk next ch, dc in last ch, turn.

Row 2: Ch 4 (counts as first dc, ch 1 throughout), [sk next ch, puff st in next dc, ch 1, sk next ch, dc in next puff st, ch 1] 3 times, sk next ch, puff st in next dc, ch 1, sk next ch, dc in last st, turn.

Row 3: Ch 4, [sk next ch, dc in next puff st, ch 1, sk next ch, puff st in next dc, ch 1] 3 times, sk next ch, dc in next puff st, ch 1, sk next ch, dc in last st, turn.

Rep rows 2 and 3 until piece measures 1½ inches, ending with row 2, fasten off.

Five O'clock

Row 1: With purple, ch 17, sc in 2nd ch from hook, [ch 5, sk each of next 4 chs, (sc, ch 3, sc) in next ch] twice, ch 5, sk each of next 4 chs, sc in last ch, turn.

Row 2: [Ch 5, (sc, ch 3, sc) in 3rd ch of ch-5 lp] 3 times, ch 2, dc in last st, turn.

Row 3: Ch 1, sc in same st as beg ch-1, [ch 5, (sc, ch 3, sc) in 3rd ch of next ch-5 sp] twice, ch 5, sc in 3rd ch of last ch-5 sp, turn.

Rows 4–7: Rep rows 2 and 3.

Row 8: Rep row 2.

Row 9: Ch 1, sc in same st as beg ch-1, [ch 5, sc in 3rd ch of next ch-5 sp] 3 times, fasten off.

Six O'clock

Row 1: With cappuccino, ch 18, dc in 4th ch from hook, dc in each rem ch across, turn. (16 dc)

Row 2: Ch 3, dc in each st across, turn.

Row 3: Ch 3, *fptrtr (see Special Stitches) around each of next 2 dc of row 1**, dc in each of next 2 dc of previous row, rep from * across, ending last rep at **, dc in last st, turn.

Row 4: Rep row 2.

Row 5: Ch 3, *fptrtr around each of next 2 fptrtr directly below**, dc in each of next 2 dc of previous row, rep from * across, ending last rep at **, dc in last st, turn.

Rows 6 & 7: Rep rows 4 and 5.

Row 8: Ch 1, sc in each st across, fasten off.

Seven O'clock

Row 1: With burgundy, ch 18, dc in 4th ch from hook, dc in each rem ch across, turn. (16 dc)

Row 2: Ch 3, dc in next dc, [ch 3, sk next 2 dc, sc in next dc, ch 3, sk next 2 dc, dc in each of next 2 dc] twice, turn.

Row 3: Ch 3, dc in next dc, [ch 5, dc in each of next 2 dc] twice, turn.

Row 4: Ch 3, dc in each dc and each ch across, turn. (16 dc)

Rows 5–7: Rep rows 2–4. At the end of row 7, fasten off.

Eight O'clock

Row 1: Thread 84 ice blue beads onto delft crochet cotton. Ch 17, sc in 2nd ch from hook, [{push up 1 bead, ch 1 over bead} 4 times, sk next 4 chs, sc in next ch] 3 times, turn.

Row 2: Ch 1, sc in same sc as beg ch-1, [ch 4, sk bead ch, sc in next sc] 3 times, turn.

Row 3: Ch 1, sc in same sc as beg

ch-1, [{push up 1 bead, ch 1 over bead} 4 times, sk next 4 chs, sc in next ch] 3 times, turn.
Rep rows 2 and 3 until piece measures 1½ inches, ending with row 2, fasten off.

Nine O'clock
Row 1: With goldenrod, ch 18, dc in 4th ch from hook, dc in each rem ch across, turn. *(16 dc)*
Row 2: Ch 3, dc in each st across, turn.
Row 3: Ch 3, dc in next st, [fptrtr around next st, dc in next st] 7 times, turn.
Row 4: Ch 3, dc in next st, [**bptrtr** *(see Special Stitches)* around next st, dc in next st] 7 times, turn.
Row 5: Rep row 2.
Rows 6–8: Rep rows 2–4.
Row 9: Ch 1, sc in each st across, fasten off.

Ten O'clock
Row 1: With forest green, ch 17, sc in 2nd ch from hook, [ch 4, sk each of next 4 chs, sc in next ch] 3 times, turn.
Row 2: Ch 5 *(counts as first dc, ch 2)*, [bullion st *(see Special Stitches)* in next ch-4 sp, ch 4] twice, bullion st in next ch-4 sp, ch 2, dc in last st, turn.
Row 3: Ch 1, sc in same st as beg ch-1, [ch 4, sc in next ch-4 sp] twice, ch 4, sc in 3rd ch of beg ch-5.
Rep rows 2 and 3 until piece measures 1½ inches, ending with row 3, fasten off.

Eleven O'clock
Row 1: With wood violet, ch 17, sc in 2nd ch from hook, sc in each rem ch across, turn. *(16 sc)*
Row 2: Ch 1, sc in first sc, [ch 3, sc in each of next 3 sc] 5 times, turn.
Row 3: Ch 1, sk all ch-3 sps, sc in each sc across, turn. *(16 sc)*
Row 4: Ch 1, sc in each of next 2 sc, [ch 3, sc in each of next 3 sc] 4 times, ch 3, sc in each of next 2 sc, turn.

Row 5: Rep row 3.
Row 6: Ch 1, [sc in each of next 3 sc, ch 3] 5 times, sc in last sc, turn.
Row 7: Rep row 3.
Rows 8–13: Rep rows 2–7.
Rows 14 & 15: Rep rows 2 and 3.
Row 16: Ch 1, sc in each sc across, fasten off.

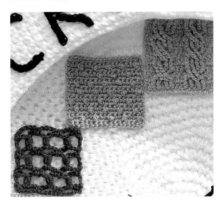

Twelve O'clock
Row 1: With camel, ch 18, dc in 4th ch from hook, dc in each rem ch across, turn. *(16 dc)*
Row 2: Ch 3, dc in next st, [**bpdtr** *(see Special Stitches)* around each of next 2 sts, dc in next st, bpdtr around each of next 2 sts, dc in each of next 2 sts] twice, turn.
Row 3: Ch 3, dc, [sk next 3 sts, fptrtr around each of next 2 sts, sc in sk dc, fptrtr around first sk st, fptrtr around next sk st, dc in each of next 2 sts] twice, turn.
Rep rows 2 and 3 until piece measures 1½ inches, ending with row 2, fasten off.
Using photo as a guide, glue each square to disk.

Crochet Time Lettering
With size 3 hook and black, work a ch the given number of times for each letter, then sl st in back ridge of each ch across, fasten off.
Using photo as a guide, shape and glue letters to ring forming the word CROCHET evenly sp across the top and TIME evenly sp across the bottom.
For crochet: C—ch 19, R—ch 31, O—ch 26, C—ch 19. H is three pieces: ch

11 for each side and ch 4 for center line. E is two pieces: ch 23 for top, side and bottom, and ch 5 for center line. T is two pieces, ch 9 each.
For Time, T *(see previous)*. I is 3 pieces: ch 9 for top and bottom and ch 7 for middle. M—ch 41. E *(see previous)*.

Basket
Row 1: With size 3 hook and cappuccino, ch 11, dc in 4th ch from hook, dc in each rem ch across, turn. *(9 dc)*
Row 2: Ch 4 *(counts as first dc, ch 1 throughout)*, dc in next dc, [ch 1, dc in next dc] across, turn. *(9 dc; 9 ch-1 sps)*
Rows 3–6: Ch 4, sk next ch, dc in next dc, [ch 1, sk next ch-1 sp, dc in next dc] across, turn. At the end of row 6, do not turn.
Row 7: Ch 1, **reverse sc** *(see illustration)* in each st across, leaving a length of cotton, fasten off.

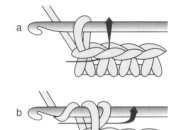

Reverse Single Crochet

Finishing
Sew sides and bottom of basket to clock ring beside 9 o'clock leaving it pouched out a little to accommodate balls of thread.
Wrap a small amount of each color thread into a ball and place in basket allowing the threads from the uppermost balls to dangle over the front of the basket. Apply glue to hold in place.
Cut 12 inches of each color thread. Holding all strands tog, tie them into a bow around steel hook to be glued to ring. Glue hook to ring beside 3 o'clock. ◆

Surf's Up!

DESIGN BY
BELINDA "BENDY" CARTER

This large, colorful cotton towel with handy pockets makes it a snap to take along those necessary items for a day at the beach. It ties up into an easy-to-carry roll complete with shoulder strap.

Beginner •

Size
Towel: 32 x 56 inches, excluding pockets

Materials
- Lion Brand Cotton-Ease medium (worsted) weight yarn (3½ oz/207 yds/100g per skein):
  - 4 skeins #148 popsicle blue
  - 3 skeins each #113 cherry red, #158 pineapple and #133 orangeade
- Sizes E/4/3.5mm and K/10½/6.5mm crochet hooks or sizes needed to obtain gauge
- Yarn needle
- Straight pins

Gauge
Size K hook: 7 sc = 3 inches; 6 rows = 3 inches
Size E hook: 13 sts = 3 inches

Pattern Notes
Weave in loose ends as work progresses.
Join rounds with a slip stitch unless otherwise stated.

Towel
Row 1: With size K hook and 2 strands of popsicle blue, ch 131, sc in 2nd ch from hook, sc in each rem ch across, turn. *(130 sc)*
Row 2: Working in **front lps** *(see Stitch Guide)*only, ch 1, sc in each st across, turn.
Rows 3–5: Rep row 2. At the end of row 5, fasten off.
Rows 6–10: With 2 strands of cherry red, rep row 2. At the end of last rep fasten off.
Rows 11–15: With 2 strands of pineapple, rep row 2. At the end of last rep, fasten off.
Rows 16–20: With 2 strands of orangeade, rep row 2. At the end of last rep, fasten off.
Rows 21–25: With 2 strands of popsicle blue, rep row 2. At the end of last rep, fasten off.
Rows 26–65: Rep rows 6–25. At the end of last rep, turn.
Row 66: Working in both lps of each sc st, ch 1, sl st in each st across, fasten off.
Row 67: Attach 2 strands of popsicle blue in opposite side of foundation ch, sl st in each ch across, fasten off.

Pocket
Make 5.
Place towel on a flat surface and fold bottom edge upward 6 inches and pin in place across edge. Working with matching yarn colors throughout, double st each vertical seam for required pocket. Stitch each outer edge of towel, double st between each of the following row groups, rows 11 and 12, rows 26 and 27, rows 41 and 42 and rows 56 and 57.
Cut 4 lengths of each color 12 inches long. Holding 1 strand of each color tog, excluding outer edge seams, attach a group of strands at top of each pocket seam, tie ends in

CONTINUED ON PAGE 113 ▶

Busy Baby

DESIGN BY
CINDY CARLSON

Beginner ●

Size
36 x 38 inches

Materials
- Red Heart Kids medium (worsted) weight yarn
  (5 oz/302 yds/141g per skein):
    16 oz each #2360 orchid and #2935 sherbet
    3 oz #2347 periwinkle
    2 oz each #2230 yellow and #2652 lime
- Size G/6/4mm crochet hook or size needed to obtain gauge
- Yarn needle
- 1-inch buttons: 2
- Music button
- Hook-and-loop tape: 6 inches
- Glue
- Tape
- Sewing needle
- Sewing thread
- 6–8 dried beans
- Empty film canister
- 4 child-safe toys
- Stitch markers
- Fiberfill

Colorful stripes cleverly worked as continuous pockets are lightly padded to create this cushiony-soft play pad for baby. Handy straps and fasteners make convenient places to attach toys, and carrying handles make it easy to take along.

Gauge
7 sc = 2 inches; 7 sc rows = 2 inches

Pattern Notes
Weave in loose ends as work progresses.
Do not join rounds unless otherwise stated; use stitch marker to mark rounds.

Play Pad
Row 1: With orchid, ch 121, sc in 2nd ch from hook, sc in each rem ch across. *(120 sc)*
Note: While working the pocket sections, use a st marker in the first st and 120th st of rnd, moving markers as work progresses.
Rnd 2 (RS): Now working in rnds, ch 1, working in **front lps** *(see Stitch Guide)* only, sc in each of next 120 sts, turn; working in rem lps of row 1, sc in each of next 120 sts, sl st to join in beg sc. *(240 sc)*
Rnd 3: Ch 1, sc in each sc around, join in beg sc. *(240 sc)*
Rnds 4–9: Rep rnd 3.
Row 10: Holding both sides tog, working through both thicknesses and stuffing pocket lightly with fiberfill as work progresses, ch 1, sc

in each of next 120 sc, fasten off.
Row 11: Attach sherbet in first sc, ch 1, sc in each sc across. *(120 sc)*
Rnds 12–19: Rep rnds 2–9.
Row 20: Rep row 10.
Row 21: Attach orchid, rep Row 11.
Rnds 22–29: Rep rnds 2–9.
Row 30: Rep row 10.
Row 31: Attach sherbet, rep row 11.
Rnds 32–39: Rep rnds 2–9.
Row 40: Rep row 10.
Row 41: Attach orchid, rep row 11.
Rnds 42–49: Rep rnds 2–9.
Row 50: Rep row 10.
Row 51: Attach sherbet, rep row 11.
Rnds 52–59: Rep rnds 2–9.
Row 60: Rep row 10.
Row 61: Attach orchid, rep row 11.
Rnds 62–69: Rep rnds 2–9.
Row 70: Rep row 10.
Row 71: Attach sherbet, rep row 11.
Rnds 72–79: Rep rnds 2–9.
Row 80: Rep row 10.
Row 81: Attach orchid, rep row 11.
Rnds 82–89: Rep rnds 2–9.
Row 90: Rep row 10.
Row 91: Attach sherbet, rep row 11.
Rnds 92–99: Rep rnds 2–9.
Row 100: Rep row 10.
Row 101: Attach orchid, rep row 11.
Rnds 102–109: Rep rnds 2–9.

100

Row 110: Rep row 10.
Row 111: Attach sherbet, rep row 11.
Rnds 112–119: Rep rnds 2–9.
Row 120: Rep row 10.
Row 121: Attach orchid, rep row 11.
Rnds 122–129: Rep rnds 2–9.
Row 130: Rep row 10, fasten off.
Edging
Note: Work edging in sts of last row of play pad and on opposite side of foundation ch of play pad.
Row 1: Attach periwinkle in first st, ch 1, sc in same st as beg ch-1, dc in next st, [sc in next st, dc in next st] across, turn. *(120 sts)*
Rows 2–4: Ch 1, sc in first dc, dc in next sc, [sc in next dc, dc in next sc] across, turn.
Row 5: Ch 1, **reverse sc** *(see illustration)* in each st across, fasten off.

Toy Strap
Make 1 each orchid, yellow, lime and periwinkle.

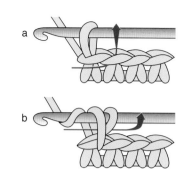

Reverse Single Crochet

Row 1: Ch 5, sc in 2nd ch from hook, sc in each of next 3 chs, turn. *(4 sc)*
Rows 2–46: Ch 1, sc in each of next 4 sc, turn. At the end of last rep, fasten off.
Ball
Make 4.
Rnd 1: With sherbet, ch 2, 6 sc in 2nd ch from hook. *(6 sc)*
Rnd 2: 2 sc in each sc around. *(12 sc)*
Rnds 3 & 4: Sc in each sc around.
Rnd 5: [Sc dec *(see Stitch Guide)* in next 2 sc, sc in next sc] 4 times. *(8 sc)*

Stuff ball with fiberfill.
Rnd 6: [Sc dec in next 2 sc] 4 times, sl st in next sc, leaving a length of yarn, fasten off.
Sew ball centered over rows 2 and 3 of toy strap. On the underside of toy strap centered over rows 2 and 3, sew a 1-inch piece of first half of hook-and-loop tape. Fold toy strap up 10 rows and sew 2nd half of hook-and-loop tape to toy strap. Sew row 46 of toy strap to row 1 of edging 4 inches from corner. Rep attaching rem straps at each rem corner in same manner. Open hook-and-loop tape and pass strap through child-safe toy and reattach hook-and-loop tape.

Flower
Center
Make 2.
Rnd 1: With yellow, ch 3, 9 hdc in first ch, sl st to join in 3rd ch of beg

ch-3. *(10 hdc)*

Rnd 2: Ch 2 *(counts as first hdc throughout)*, hdc in same st as beg ch, 2 hdc in each hdc around, join in 2nd ch of beg ch-2. *(20 hdc)*

Rnd 3: Ch 2, hdc in same st as beg ch, hdc in next st, [2 hdc in next st, hdc in next st] around, join in second ch of beg ch-2. *(30 hdc)*

Rnd 4: Rep rnd 3, fasten off. *(45 hdc)*

Rnd 5: With WS of centers tog and working through both thicknesses, attach sherbet, ch 1, sc in same sc as beg ch-1, sc in each st around, stuffing lightly with fiberfill before closing, sl st to join in beg sc. *(45 sc)*

Petals

Rnd 6: [Ch 2, sk 2 sc, sl st in next sc] around. *(15 ch-2 lps)*

Rnd 7: Ch 1, (sc, hdc, 3 dc, hdc, sc) in each ch-2 sp around, join in beg sc, fasten off. *(15 petals)*

Music button holder

Rnd 1: With lime, ch 2, 6 sc in 2nd ch from hook. *(6 sc)*

Rnd 2: 2 sc in each sc around. *(12 sc)*

Rnd 3: [2 sc in next sc, sc in next sc] around. *(18 sc)*

Rnd 4: Sc in each sc around.

Rnd 5: Rep rnd 4, sl st in next sc, leaving a length of yarn, fasten off. Holding music button in center of music button holder, sew to center front of flower.

Sew a 1-inch piece of hook-and-loop tape to underside of flower. Sew 2nd half of hook-and-loop tape on same edge as toy straps centered between them. Press flower in place.

Rattle

Note: Place dry beans in empty film canister, glue cover to container and wrap container with tape.

Rnd 1: With sherbet, ch 2, 6 sc in 2nd ch from hook. *(6 sc)*

Rnd 2: 2 sc in each sc around. *(12 sc)*

Rnd 3: [2 sc in next sc, sc in next sc] around. *(18 sc)*

Rnd 4: Working in **back lps** *(see Stitch Guide)* for this rnd only, sc in

each st around.

Rnds 5–13: Sc in each sc around.

Rnd 14: Rep rnd 4, lightly stuff with fiberfill, leaving a hole in middle and insert film canister, add a small amount of fiberfill on top of canister.

Rnd 15: [Sc dec in next 2 sc, sc in next sc] around. *(12 sc)*

Rnd 16: [Sc dec in next 2 sc] 6 times. *(6 sc)*

Rnd 17: [Sc dec in next 2 sc, sc in next sc] twice, sl st in next st, leaving a length of yarn, fasten off. Sew opening closed.

Tassel

Make 1 each yellow, lime and periwinkle.

Row 1: Ch 21, 3 sc in 2nd ch from hook, 3 sc in each rem ch across, leaving a length of yarn, fasten off. Sew the 3 tassels over rnd 17 of rattle. Sew a 1-inch piece hook-

and-loop tape to center of rattle. Sew rem half of hook-and-loop tape centered at opposite edging of flower. Press rattle into place.

Carrying Handles

Make 2.

Note: Child safety warning: The handles could become a safety hazard to small children. It is imperative that 1-inch buttons are used on the underside of play pad to secure handles before playtime.

Row 1: With periwinkle, ch 5, sc in 2nd ch from hook, dc in next ch, sc in next ch, dc in last ch, turn. *(4 sts)*

Row 2: Ch 1, [sc in next dc, dc in next sc] twice, turn. *(4 sts)*

Rows 3–17: Rep row 2.

Row 18: Ch 1, sc in each of next 4 sts, turn. *(4 sc)*

Row 19: Ch 1, sl st in first sc, ch

CONTINUED ON PAGE 113 ▶

Creature Comforts

DESIGNS BY
KATHLEEN STUART

These adorable critters, cleverly disguised as hot water bottle covers, are ready to give quick, soothing comfort to a child. They also make cute pajama bags!

Easy ••

Size
Lamb: 15 x 16 inches; fits rectangular 2-quart capacity hot water bottle

Materials
- Lion Brand Jiffy bulky (chunky) weight yarn (3 oz/135 yds/85g per skein):
    2 skeins #099 fisherman
- Medium (worsted) weight yarn (3 oz/170 yds/85g per skein):
    1 oz black
    1 yd each light blue and pale pink
- Size J/10/6mm crochet hook or size needed to obtain gauge
- Yarn needle
- Sewing needle
- Sewing thread
- 6 x 12-inch rectangular water bottle
- ½-inch snap fastener
- Stitch marker

Lamb

Gauge
3 sts = 1 inch
Check gauge to save time.

Pattern Notes
Weave in loose ends as work progresses.
Do not join rounds unless otherwise stated. Use a stitch marker to mark rounds.

Head
Rnd 1: With black, ch 2, 6 sc in 2nd ch from hook. *(6 sc)*
Rnd 2: [Sc in next st, 2 sc in next st] around. *(9 sc)*
Rnd 3: [Sc in each of next 2 sts, 2 sc in next st] around. *(12 sc)*
Rnd 4: Rep rnd 2. *(18 sc)*
Rnd 5: Rep rnd 3. *(24 sc)*
Rnd 6: [Sc in each of next 3 sts, 2 sc in next st] around. *(30 sc)*
Rnds 7 & 8: Sc in each sc around. At the end of rnd 8, draw up a lp of fisherman, fasten off black.
Rnd 9: [{Sc in next st, tr in next st} twice, (sc, tr) in next st] around. *(36 sts)*
Rnd 10: [Tr in next st, sc in next st] around.
Rnd 11: [Sc in next st, tr in next st] around.

Rnd 12: Rep rnd 10.
Rnd 13: [Sc in next tr, tr in next st, sc in next st, tr in next st, **sc dec** *(see Stitch Guide)* in next 2 sts] around. *(30 sts)*
Rnd 14: [Tr in next st, sc in next st, sc dec in next 2 sts] around. *(24 sts)*

Body
Rnd 15: Draw up a lp, remove hook. Using length of yarn from opposite end of skein, attach fisherman with a sl st in 13th st of rnd 14, ch 5, fasten off. Pick up dropped lp, ch 6, sc in 2nd ch from hook, sc in each of next 4 chs, sc in each of next 12 sts on rnd 14, sc in next 4 chs, 3 sc in last ch, working on opposite side of ch, sc in next 4 chs, sc in same st as sl st on rnd 14, sc in next 11 sts on rnd 14, sc in next 4 chs, 2 sc in same ch as beg sc, do not join. *(46 sts)*
Rnd 16: [Sc in next st, tr in next st] around.
Rnds 17: [Tr in next st, sc in next st] around.
Rnds 18–37: Rep rnds 16 and 17.
Rnds 38: Working in **back lps** *(see Stitch Guide)* only, [sc in next st, tr in next st] around.
Rnd 39: [Tr in next st, sc in next st] around, sl st in next st, fasten off.

Flap

Rnd 1: Working in rem front lps of rnd 37, join fisherman in 24th st, ch 24, join with sc in first st on rnd 37, tr in next st, [sc in next st, tr in next st] 10 times, working across ch, [sc in next st, tr in next st] 12 times. *(46 sts)*

Rnd 2: [Tr in next st, sc in next st] around.

Rnd 3: [Sc in next st, tr in next st] around.

Rnds 4 & 5: Rep rnds 2 and 3.

Rnd 6: Rep rnd 2.

Row 7: Now working in rows, flatten piece across. Working through both thicknesses in top lps only, sl st in each st across, fasten off.

With sewing needle and thread, sew snap fastener at center of flap and body opening.

Ear

Make 2.

Rnd 1: With fisherman, ch 2, 6 sc in 2nd ch from hook. *(6 sc)*

Rnd 2: 2 sc in each of next 3 sts, change to black, 2 sc in each of next 3 sts, change to fisherman. *(12 sc)*

Rnds 3–6: Sc in each of next 6 sts, change to black, sc in each of next 6 sts, change to fisherman. At the end of rnd 6, leaving a length of yarn, fasten off. With black section facing forward, flatten each ear and sew to each side of head between rnds 11 and 12.

Leg

Make 4.

Rnd 1: With black, ch 2, 6 sc in 2nd ch from hook. *(6 sc)*

Rnd 2: 2 sc in each sc around. *(12 sc)*

Rnd 3: [Sc in next sc, 2 sc in next sc] around. *(18 sc)*

Rnds 4–6: Sc in each sc around. At the end of rnd 6, change to fisherman, fasten off black.

Rnd 7: [Sc in next st, tr in next st] around.

Rnd 8: [Tr in next st, sc in next st] around.

Rnds 9 & 10: Rep rnds 7 and 8.

Rnd 11: Rep rnd 7.

Rnd 12: [Tr in next st, sc dec in next 2 sts tog] around, leaving a length of yarn, fasten off. *(12 sts)* Using photo as a guide for placement, flatten rnd 12 of leg, sew leg to body.

Facial Features

Using photo as a guide, with pale pink yarn, embroider nose in **satin stitch** *(see illustration)* over upper side of rnds 1 and 2, and embroider mouth with **straight stitches** *(see illustration)* centered below nose.

With light blue, embroider eyes evenly sp centered above nose with satin stitch.

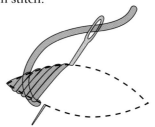

Satin Stitch

Straight Stitch

Bear

Gauge

3 sts = 1 inch
Check gauge to save time.

Pattern Notes

Weave in loose ends as work progresses.

Do not join rounds unless otherwise stated. Use a stitch marker to mark rounds.

Head

Rnd 1: Starting at snout with deco yarn, ch 2, 6 sc in 2nd ch from hook. *(6 sc)*

Rnd 2: 2 sc in each st around. *(12 sc)*

Size

Bear: 13 x 13¼ inches; fits rectangular 1-quart capacity hot water bottle

Materials

- Lion Brand Homespun bulky (chunky) weight yarn (6 oz/ 185 yds/170g per skein):
    1 skein #318 sierra
    ¼ oz #309 deco
- Medium (worsted) weight yarn:
    1 yd black
- Size J/10/6mm crochet hook or size needed to obtain gauge
- Yarn needle
- Sewing needle
- Sewing thread
- 5 x 8½-inch hot water bottle
- ½-inch snap fastener
- Stitch marker

Rnd 3: [Sc in next st, 2 sc in next st] around. *(18 sc)*

Rnd 4: Sc in each st around.

Rnd 5: Rep rnd 4, changing to sierra in last st.

Rnd 6: Working in **back lps** *(see Stitch Guide)* only, [sc in each of next 2 sts, 2 sc in next st] around. *(24 sc)*

Rnd 7: [Sc in each of next 3 sts, 2 sc in next st] around. *(30 sc)*

Rnds 8–11: Rep rnd 4.

Rnd 12: [Sc in each of next 2 sts, **sc dec** *(see Stitch Guide)* in next 2 sts]

around. *(24 sc)*
Rnd 13: [Sc in each of next 2 sts, sc dec in next 2 sts] around. *(18 sc)*

Body

Rnd 14: Draw up a lp, remove hook, working with a length of yarn from opposite end of skein, attach sierra with a sl st in 10th st, ch 4, fasten off. Pick up dropped lp, ch 5, sc in 2nd ch from hook, sc in each of next 3 chs, sc in each of next 9 sts on rnd 13, sc in each of next 3 chs, 3 sc in last ch, working on opposite side of ch, sc in each of next 3 chs, sc in same st as sl st on rnd 13, sc in each of next 8 sts on rnd 13, sc in each of next 3 chs, 2 sc in same ch as beg sc. *(36 sc)*
Rnds 15–34: Rep rnd 4.
Rnd 35: Working in back lps only, sc in each st around.
Rnd 36: Sc in each st around, sl st in next st, fasten off.

Flap

Rnd 1: Working in rem **front lps** *(see Stitch Guide)* of rnd 34, attach sierra in 18th st on rnd 34, ch 18, join with sc in first st of rnd 34, sc in each of next 18 sts, sc in each of next 18 chs. *(36 sc)*
Rnds 2–6: Sc in each st around.
Row 7: Now working in rows, flatten sides, working in top lps only through both thicknesses, sl st in each st across, fasten off.
With sewing needle and thread, sew snap fastener at center of flap and body opening.

Ear

Make 2.
Rnd 1: With sierra, ch 2, 5 sc in 2nd ch from hook. *(5 sc)*
Rnd 2: 2 sc in each st around. *(10 sc)*
Rnd 3: [Sc in next st, 2 sc in next st] around. *(15 sc)*
Rnd 4: Sc in each st around.
Rnd 5: Rep rnd 4, sl st in next st, leaving a length of yarn, fasten off.
Flatten ear and sew ear to side of head

between rnds 11 and 12. Rep with rem ear on opposite side of head.

Leg

Make 4.
Rnd 1: With sierra, ch 2, 5 sc in 2nd ch from hook. *(5 sc)*
Rnd 2: 2 sc in each st around. *(10 sc)*
Rnd 3: [Sc in next st, 2 sc in next st] around. *(15 sc)*
Rnds 4–12: Sc in each sc around.
Rnd 13: [Sc in next st, sc dec in next 2 sts] around, sl st in next st, leaving a length of yarn, fasten off. *(10 sc)*
Using photo as a guide for placement, flatten rnd 13 of leg and sew each leg to body.

Facial Features

Using photo as a guide, with black, embroider nose and mouth in satin stitch over rnds 1 and 2 of snout. With black, embroider eyes of rnd 6 of head centered above nose.

Turtle

Easy ●●

Size

Turtle: 10 x 11½ inches; fits 6" round hot water bottle

Materials

- Lion Brand Homespun bulky (chunky) weight yarn (6 oz/ 185 yds/170g per skein):
    1 skein #369 Florida keys green
- Lion Brand Boucle bulky (chunky) weight yarn (2½ oz/57 yds/70g per skein):
    1 skein #202 lime blue
- Size J/10/6mm crochet hook or size needed to obtain gauge
- Yarn needle
- Sewing needle
- Sewing thread
- ½-inch snap fastener
- 6½ x 8½-inch round water bottle
- Stitch marker

Gauge

3 sts = 1 inch
Check gauge to save time.

Pattern Notes

Weave in loose ends as work progresses.
Do not join rounds unless otherwise stated. Use a stitch marker to mark rounds.

Head

Rnd 1: With Florida keys green, ch 2, 6 sc in 2nd ch from hook. *(6 sc)*
Rnd 2: 2 sc in each sc around. *(12 sc)*
Rnd 3: [Sc in next st, 2 sc in next st] around. *(18 sc)*
Rnd 4: [Sc in each of next 2 sts, 2 sc in next st] around. *(24 sc)*
Rnd 5: Sc in each sc around.
Rnd 6–9: Rep rnd 5.
Rnd 10: [Sc in each of next 2 st, **sc dec** *(see Stitch Guide)* in next 2 sts] around. *(18 sc)*
Rnd 11: [Sc in next st, sc dec in next 2 sts] around. *(12 sc)*

Body

Rnd 12: Rep rnd 2. *(24 sc)*
Rnd 13: [Sc in each of next 3 sts, 2 sc in next st] around. *(30 sts)*
Rnd 14: [Sc in each of next 4 sts, 2 sc in next st] around. *(36 sts)*
Rnds 15 & 16: Rep rnd 5.
Rnd 17: Sc in each of next 8 sts, 2 sc in each of next 2 sts, sc in each of next 16 sts, 2 sc in each of next 2 sts, sc in each of next 8 sts. *(40 sc)*
Rnds 18–24: Sc in each st around.

Rnd 25: Sc in each of next 8 sts, [sc dec in next 2 sts] twice, sc in each of next 16 sts, [sc dec in each of next 2 sts] twice, sc in each of next 8 sts. *(36 sc)*

Rnd 26: [Sc in each of next 4 sts, sc dec in next 2 sts] around. *(30 sts)*

Rnd 27: Working in back lps only, [sc in each of next 3 sts, sc dec in next 2 sts] around. *(24 sc)*

Rnd 28: [Sc in each of next 2 sts, sc dec in next 2 sc] around. *(18 sc)*

Rnd 29: Sc in each st around, sl st in next st, fasten off.

Flap

Rnd 1: Working in rem front lps of rnd 26, attach Florida keys green with sl st in 26th st on rnd 26, ch 15, join with sc in 10th st on rnd 26, sc in each of next 15 sts, working in chs, sc in each of next 15 chs. *(30 sc)*

Rnd 2: [Sc in each of next 3 sts, sc dec in next 2 sts] around. *(24 sts)*

Rnd 3: [Sc in each of next 2 sts, sc dec in next 2 sts] around. *(18 sc)*

Rnd 4: [Sc in next st, sc dec in next 2 sts] around. *(12 sc)*

Row 5: Now working in rows, flatten side, working in top lps, sl st in each st across, fasten off. With sewing needle and thread, sew snap fastener center of flap and body opening.

Leg

Make 4.

Rnd 1: With Florida keys green, ch 2, 6 sc in 2nd ch from hook. *(6 sc)*

Rnd 2: 2 sc in each st around. *(12 sc)*

Rnd 3: Sc in each st around.

Rnd 4: Rep rnd 3.

Rnd 5: [Sc dec in next 2 sts] 6 times. *(6 sc)*

Rnds 6 & 7: Rep rnd 3. At the end of rnd 7, leaving a length of yarn, fasten off. Using photo as a guide, flatten rnd 7 of leg and sew to body.

Tail

Rnd 1: With Florida keys green, ch 2, 6 sc in 2nd ch from hook. *(6 sc)*

Rnd 2: [Sc in next st, 2 sc in next st] around. *(9 sc)*

Rnds 3 & 4: Sc in each st around. At the end of Rnd 4, leaving a length of yarn, fasten off. Flatten rnd 4 and sew tail to back end of turtle.

Pentagon Shell Motif

Make 6.

Rnd 1: With lime blue, ch 4, sl st to join in first ch to form a ring, ch 3 *(counts as first dc throughout)*, 2 dc in ring, [ch 2, 3 dc in ring] 4 times, ch 2, sl st to join in 3rd ch of beg ch-3, fasten off. *(15 dc; 5 ch-2 sps)*

To form shell, crochet motifs tog by placing 2 motifs WS tog and working through both thicknesses, sc in top lps of motifs. Crochet motifs tog with 1 motif at center and 5 around outer edge of the single center motif. Shell will not lie flat. Sew shell to center top of body.

Facial Features

With black yarn, embroider satin st eyes between rnds 3 and 4 of head. ◆

Travel Neck Soother CONTINUED FROM PAGE 78 ▶

row 30 to center matching ch-2 sps, working through both thicknesses, attach baby aqua in first ch-2 sp, ch 1, 3 sc in same ch-2 sp, 3 sc in each of next 3 ch-2 sps, turn. *(12 sc)*

Rows 2–4: Ch 1, sc in each of next 12 sc, turn.

Row 5: Ch 1, sc in each of next 5 sc, 2 sc in next sc, sc in each of next 6 sc, turn. *(13 sc)*

Row 6: Ch 1, sc in same sc as beg ch-1, [ch 2, sk next sc, sc in next sc] 6 times, turn. *(7 sc; 6 ch-2 sps)*

Row 7: Sl st into ch-2 sp, ch 1, sc in same ch-2 sp, [ch 3, sc in next ch-2 sp] 5 times, turn. *(6 sc; 5 ch-3 sps)*

Row 8: Ch 1, sc in same sc as beg ch-1, shell in next ch-3 sp, [sc in next ch-3 sp, shell in next ch-3 sp] twice, sc in last sc, turn. *(4 sc; 3 shells)*

Rows 9–19: Ch 1, sc in first sc, [shell in 3rd dc of shell, sc in next sc] 3 times, turn. At the end of row 19, fasten off.

Second End Tie

Row 1: Using care to place proper side facing, place crochet cover on a flat surface the same side as previously completed tie, fold each side edge of opposite side of foundation ch to center matching ch-2 sps, working through both thicknesses, attach baby aqua in first ch-2 sp, ch 1, 3 sc in same ch-2 sp, 3 sc in each of next 3 ch-2 sps, turn. *(12 sc)*

Rows 2–19: Rep rows 2–19 of first end tie.

Holding Loop

With 2nd end tie facing, attach baby aqua in side edge of row 5, ch 10, sl st in opposite edge of the same row 5, ch 1, work 12 sc over ch-10, sl st in first ch, fasten off.

Finishing

Sew a button to edge of each row 10 and 20 of crochet cover. Use natural sps on opposite edge for buttonholes.

To use neck soother, rice fabric roll *(hot)* should be heated in the microwave and the watersorb fabric roll *(cold)* should be soaked in cold water until it swells. Insert pieces into crochet cover, button and place around neck. For storage, allow hot pack to cool and wet pack to dry, insert back into crochet cover. ◆

Two-in-One Games CONTINUED FROM PAGE 70 ▶

Tail

Row 8: Now working in rows, ch 37, sl st in 2nd ch from hook, sl st in each rem ch across, leaving a length of yarn, fasten off.

With rem length of yarn and yarn needle, weave through rem sts of rnd 7, pull tightly, knot to secure. Alternating color of checkers, string checkers onto tail. Tie end of tail in a soft knot.

Finishing

With sewing needle and black thread, sew eyes to rnd 2 of head. Skipping center 2 sc at top of head, insert chenille stem at right, under next 2 sc and out again. Bend each end of stem to form antennae. Glue base of each antennae. Glue a red pompom to top of each antennae.

Tote Bag

Tic-Tac-Toe Board

Row 1: With skipper blue, ch 49, sc in 2nd ch from hook, sc in each rem ch across, turn. *(48 sc)*

Rows 2–48: Ch 1, sc in each sc across, turn.

Make 2 lines of ch sts across, spaced 16 rows apart, 1 each from orange and yellow. Make 2 lines of ch sts down, spaced 16 sc apart, 1 each red and emerald green.

Border

Rnd 1: Attach black to outer edge of board, ch 1, sc evenly sp around outer edge, working 3 sc in each corner st, join in beg sc, fasten off.

Checkerboard

Note: To change color: Work last sc until 2 lps rem on hook, with new color, yo, draw through rem 2 lps on hook.

Row 1: With skipper blue, ch 49, sc in 2nd ch from hook, sc in each of next 5 chs, with maize, sc in each of next 6 chs, [with skipper blue, sc in each of next 6 chs, with maize, sc in each of next 6 chs] 3 times, turn. *(8 blocks; 48 sc)*

Row 2: Ch 1, [with maize, sc in each of next 6 sc, with skipper blue, sc in each of next 6 sc] 4 times, turn.

Row 3: Ch 1, [with skipper blue, sc in each of next 6 sc, with maize, sc in each of next 6 sc] 4 times, turn.

Row 4: Rep row 2.

Row 5: Rep row 3.

Row 6: Rep row 2.

Rows 7–12: Rep rows 2 and 3 in that order to reverse block colors. At the end of row 12, draw up a lp of skipper blue, turn.

Rows 13–18: Rep rows 3 and 2 in that order to reverse block colors. At the end of row 18, draw up a lp of maize, turn.

Rows 19–48: Rep rows 7–18. At the end of row 48, fasten off. Board has a total of 64 blocks, 8 x 8.

Border

Rnd 1: Attach black to outer edge of board, ch 1, sc evenly sp around outer edge, working 3 sc in each corner st, join in beg sc, fasten off.

Joining Boards

Row 1: With WS of boards tog, attach black in any center corner sc and, working through both thicknesses, ch 1, sc in same st as beg ch-1, sc evenly sp across to within next center corner sc, [2 sc in center corner sc, sc evenly sp across to within next center corner sc] twice, ending with 1 sc in next center corner sc, do not turn.

Rnd 2: Now working in rnds, ch 1, working around top opening of tote, sc evenly sp around entire edge, join in beg sc, fasten off.

Handle

Make 2.

Row 1: With jockey red, ch 37, sc in 2nd ch from hook, sc in each rem ch across, turn. *(36 sc)*

Rows 2–4: Ch 1, sc in each sc across, turn. At the end of row 4, fasten off.

With black sewing thread and needle, allowing a 3½ inch sp between each end of handle, sew ends of handle to inside of top opening. ◆

Scrapbooking Keeper CONTINUED FROM PAGE 76 ▶

rows to row 14 of navy pocket and with button lp at opposite edge, whipstitch side edge of flap rows to row 14 of navy pocket.

Sew button to center front of Spanish red pocket between rows 7 and 8. ◆

next 2 sts, sc in last st, turn. *(9 shells)*

Rows 4–29: Rep rows 2 and 3. At the end of last rep, fasten off.

Handle

Make 2.

Row 1: With light teal, ch 60, dc in 4th ch from hook, dc in each rem ch across, turn. *(58 dc)*

Rnd 2: Now working in rnds around outer edge, sl st in each st and 2 sl sts in end of each end of row, join with sl st in first sl st, fasten off.

Appliqués

Basket

Row 1: With honey gold, ch 35, dc in 4th ch from hook, dc in each rem ch across, turn. *(33 dc)*

Rows 2–8: Ch 3, dc in each of next 2 sts, **fpdc** *(see Special Stitches)* around each of next 3 sts, ***bpdc** *(see Special Stitches)* around each of next 3 sts, fpdc around each of next 3 sts, rep from * across, turn. At the end of last rep, fasten off.

Basket Handle

With honey gold, ch 96, dc in 5th ch from hook, dc back into 4th ch from hook, [sk next ch, dc in next ch, dc in sk ch] across, fasten off.

Collar

With peacock green, ch 15, sl st in 2nd ch from hook, sl st in each

rem ch across, fasten off. *(14 sl sts)* Sew jingle bell to collar.

Ball of Yarn

Make 1 peacock green, 1 young pink and 2 grenadine.

Note: Do not join rnds, use st marker to mark rnds.

Rnd 1: Ch 2, 6 sc in 2nd ch from hook. *(6 sc)*

Rnd 2: 2 sc in each st around. *(12 sc)*

Rnd 3: [Sc in next st, 2 sc in next st] around. *(18 sc)*

Rnd 4: [Sc in each of next 2 sts, 2 sc in next st] around. *(24 sc)*

Rnd 5: [Sc in each of next 3 sts, 2 sc in next st] around, fasten off. *(30 sc)*

Kitten

Row 1: Starting at bottom, with size H hook and white, ch 16, sc in 2nd ch from hook, sc in each rem ch across, turn. *(15 sc)*

Row 2: Ch 1, sc in each st across, turn.

Rows 3–11: Rep row 2.

Row 12: Ch 1, **sc dec** *(see Stitch Guide)* in next 2 sc, sc in each rem st across, turn. *(14 sc)*

Row 13: Ch 1, sc in each st across to last 2 sts, sc dec in last 2 sts, turn. *(13 sc)*

Rows 14 & 15: Rep rows 12 and 13. *(11 sc)*

Rows 16 & 17: Ch 1, sc dec in next 2 sc, sc in each st across to last 2 sts, sc dec in last 2 sts, turn. *(7 sc)*

Row 18: Rep row 2.

Rows 19 & 20: Ch 1, 2 sc in

first st, sc in each st across to last st, 2 sc in last st, turn. *(11 sts)*

Rows 21–24: Rep row 2.

First ear

Row 25: Ch 1, sc in each of next 4 sts, leaving rem sts unworked, turn. *(4 sc)*

Row 26: Ch 1, [sc dec in next 2 sts] twice, turn. *(2 sc)*

Row 27: Ch 1, sc dec in next 2 sts, fasten off, do not turn.

Second ear

Row 25: Sk next 3 sts on row 24, attach white in next st, ch 1, sc in same st as beg ch-1, sc in each of next 3 sts, turn. *(4 sc)*

Rows 26 & 27: Rep rows 26 and 27 of first ear.

With peacock green, using French knot, embroider eyes 1¼ inches apart on rnd 23. With grenadine using French knot and straight sts, embroider nose and mouth. With 6 strands of black embroidery floss, using straight sts, embroider whiskers.

Finishing

1. For front, sew ball of yarn No. 1 on one side 2½ inches from right edge over rnds 10–14.

2. With matching yarn, using long straight sts, embroider ball

Cat Facial Illustration

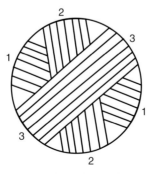

Embroidery Illustration

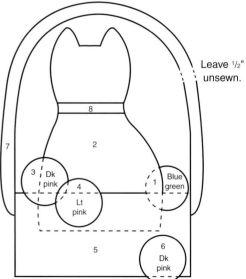

Leave ¹/₂" unsewn.

Cat Sewing Illustration

of yarn according to embroidery illustration.

3. Sew matching appliqués on side in order according to sewing illustration; embroider each ball of yarn.

4. Run ribbon through unsewn ½ inch on basket handle, tie in bow.

Assembly

With front side facing, hold both tote sides WS tog, matching sts and rows; working through both thicknesses, join light teal with sc in top left corner, sc in end of each sc row and 2 sc in end of each dc row around to top right corner with 3 sc in each bottom corner, fasten off.

Sew each end of 1 handle 5 inches apart to top edge on side front. Rep with 2nd handle on back. ◆

Jazzy Gems CONTINUED FROM PAGE 84 ▶

and size N hook, ch 50, insert hook in 2nd ch from hook, yo, draw up a lp, [insert hook in next ch, yo, draw up a lp] across *(50 lps on hook)*, to work off lps, yo, draw through first lp on hook, [yo, draw through 2 lps on hook] across.

Row 2: Sk first vertical bar, [insert hook under next vertical bar, yo, draw up a lp and draw through st on hook] across, leaving a length of yarn, fasten off.

Assembly

To create each bag bottom corner and flat bottom, st ends of rows 27–30 to top of the 3 side columns of vertical bars. Matching top edge, rows of tps and corner seams, st around one side, bottom and the other side to create the bag. Position the end of one strap 8 bars from the seam, so that the end will be stitched across bars 8–10 with the flat side toward the outside of the bag. Whipstitch in place. Using photo as a guide, rep for all other ends.

Fun Fur Trim

With size J hook, attach sapphire with sl st into the vertical bar just above the top tps row, next to one seam, ch 3, dc in vertical bar, [2 dc in next vertical bar] around, treating the whipstitch as a vertical bar at each side, sl st to join in third ch of beg ch-3, fasten off. ◆

Watermelon Backpack CONTINUED FROM PAGE 92 ▶

turn. Work 22 sc over ch-19 lp, sl st in beg sc post. Work **reverse sc** *(see illustration on page 92)* across handle, sl st in same post, fasten off.

Strap

Make 2.

Row 1: With 2 strands of black, ch 8, sc in 2nd ch from hook, sc in each rem ch across, turn. *(7 sc)*

Row 2: Ch 1, sc in each sc across, turn.

Rep row 2 until strap measures 20 inches.

Work row of **reverse sc** *(see illustration on page 92)* along long side, across end and other long side, fasten off.

Center the straps *(ends without reverse sc)* on the back of the bag at the lower edge so that they meet; secure in place. Join the tops to the same black sc row as pink sts so that the edge of the straps are even with sides of the flap.

Insert the plastic canvas or the cardboard into the bag to reinforce the base bottom. ◆

next 3 chs, dc in next ch, sc in next ch] twice, in 7 unused chs [sc in next ch, dc in next ch, tr in each of next 3 chs, dc in next ch, sc in next ch] rep from * across, fasten off.

Edging

Rnd 1: Attach dark ecru to tip of first petal along either edge, *[ch 5, sc in tip of next petal, ch 1, sc in tip of next petal] 3 times, ch 5, sc in tip of petal, ch 11, sc in tip of end petal, ch 11 *, sc in tip of first petal on other side, rep from * to *, ending with sl st in first ch.
Rnd 2: Ch 5 *(counts as first dc, ch 2)*, [sk 2 sts, *dc in next st, ch 2, sk next 2 sts, dc in next st, ch 2, dc in ch between petals, ch 2, sk sc and 2 chs*, rep from * to * twice, dc in next st, ch 2, sk next 2 chs, dc in next st, ch 2, dc in next sc, ch 2, sk next 2 chs, dc in next st, ch 2, sk next 2 chs, (dc, ch 2, dc) in next st, ch 2, sk next 2 chs, dc in next st, ch 2, dc in sc, ch 2, sk next 2 chs, dc in next st, ch 2, sk next 2 chs, (dc, ch 2, dc) in next st, ch 2, sk next 2 chs, dc in next st, ch 2, dc in next sc] around, ending with ch 2, join in 3rd ch of beg ch-5, fasten off.

Finishing

Using photo as a guide, glue decorative paper to cream card with glue stick. Use glue stick to glue flowers to decorative paper. Use straight pins to hold crochet piece in position until dry. Apply a small amount of white glue to each 6mm bead and place a bead in the center of each flower.

Rose

Rnd 1: With pink, ch 6, sl st to join in beg sc to form a ring, ch 5 *(counts as first dc, ch 2)*, [dc in ring, ch 2] 7 times, join in 3rd ch of beg ch-5. *(8 dc; 8 ch-2 sps)*
Rnd 2: Ch 1, (sc, dc, tr, dc, sc) in each ch-2 sp around, join in beg sc, turn. *(8 petals)*
Note: *When two sc sts from two adjacent petals of previous rnd come tog to form a "V" over the dc below, insert hook as indicated in this area.*
Rnd 3: Ch 3, [sl st under V, ch 3] around, turn. *(8 ch-3 sps)*
Rnd 4: Ch 1, (sc, hdc, dc, tr, dc, hdc sc) in each ch-3 sp around, join in beg sc, turn. *(8 petals)*
Rnd 5: Ch 4, [sl st in V, ch 3] around, join, turn. *(8 ch-4 sps)*
Rnd 6: Ch 1, (sc, hdc, dc, 3 tr, dc, hdc, sc) in each ch-4 sp around, join in beg sc, fasten off.

Leaves

Rnd 7: Attach green in any V between two petals, *(ch 7, sc in 2nd ch from hook, hdc in next ch, dc in each of next 3 chs, hdc in next ch, sl st in same V) for small leaf, (ch 11, sc in 2nd ch from hook, hdc in next ch, dc in each of next 7 chs, hdc in next ch, sl st in same V) for large leaf, (ch 7, sc in 2nd ch from hook, hdc in next ch, dc in each of next 3 chs, hdc in next ch, sl st in same V) for small leaf, ch 3, sl st in next V, make a small leaf, ch 3, sl st in next V, rep from * around, join in base of first small leaf, fasten off.

Border

Rnd 8: Attach white in tip of any large leaf, ch 1, sc in same st as beg ch-1, [ch 5, sc in tip of next leaf] around, ending with sl st in beg sc. *(16 ch-5 sps)*
Rnd 9: Ch 7 *(counts as first dc, ch 4)*, dc in same st as beg ch-7, *[5 dc in next ch-5 sp, dc in next sc] 3 times, 5 dc in next ch-5 sp**, (dc, ch 4, dc) in corner sc, rep from * around, ending last rep at **, join in 3rd ch of beg ch-7.
Rnd 10: Sl st into corner ch-4 sp,

ch 4 *(counts as first tr)*, (2 tr, ch 2, 3 tr, ch 3, 3 tr, ch 2, 3 tr) in same ch-4 sp as beg ch-4, *[(3 tr, ch 2, 3 tr) in next dc above next leaf tip] 3 times**, (3 tr, ch 2, 3 tr, ch 3, 3 tr, ch 2, 3 tr) in corner ch-4 sp, rep from * around, ending last rep at **, join in 4th ch of beg ch-4, fasten off.
Using white glue and photo as a guide, glue rose motif to pink card.

Forget-Me-Not
Flower
Make 5.

Rnd 1: With yellow, ch 6, sl st in first ch to form a ring, ch 1, 10 sc in ring, join in beg sc, fasten off. *(10 sc)*
Rnd 2: Attach blue in any sc, *(ch 4, 3 tr, ch 4, sl st) in same sc, sl st in each of next 2 sc, rep from * 4 times, fasten off. *(5 petals)*
Using photo as a guide for placement of flowers, make rem 4 flowers the same as the first flower except: when working the 3 tr sts of petal, work 2 tr, remove hook, insert hook in center tr of adjacent petal of previous flower, pick up dropped lp and draw through st on hook, tr in same sc on working flower to complete 3-tr group of petal.

Header

Row 1: With WS of flowers facing, working across top of 3-flower edge across 2 top petals of each flower, with blue, ch 10, sl st in center tr of 3-tr group, *ch 5, sl st in center tr of 3-tr group of next petal of same flower**, ch 6, sl st in center tr of next 3-tr group of next flower, rep from * across, ending last rep at **, ch 12, turn.
Row 2: Dc in 3rd ch from hook, dc in each st across edge, fasten off.

Finishing

From white card, from lower right corner of card, measure 4½ inches from corner inward on each side, cut this triangle from card. Block and starch flowers to fit in sp of triangle. Glue header of flowers to cut edge of card. ◆

Surf's Up CONTINUED FROM PAGE 98 ▶

a bow and trim ends evenly.

Strap
Row 1: With size E hook and 1 strand popsicle blue, ch 131, sc in 2nd ch from hook, sc in each rem ch across, fasten off, turn. *(130 sc)*
Row 2: Attach cherry red in first sc, ch 1, sc in each sc across, fasten off, turn.
Row 3: With pineapple, rep row 2.
Row 4: With orangeade, rep row 2.
Row 5: With popsicle blue, rep row 2, do not fasten off, turn.
Row 6: Sl st in each sc across, fasten off.

Row 7: Attach popsicle blue in opposite side of foundation ch, sl st in each ch across, fasten off.

Tie
Make 2.
Row 1: With size K hook, holding 1 strand each of cherry red, pineapple and orangeade tog, ch 63, pick up strap and sl st across short end of strap, ch 63, fasten off. Rep row 1 working sl st across opposite end of strap.

Finishing
Place towel on a flat surface with pockets facing downward. Working at opposite end of pockets, pin each end of strap at top edge to each rows 40 and 58. With matching yarn, sew each end of strap to towel.
Fold towel in half lengthwise with strap and ties on the underside and starting at bottom pocket edge, roll towel up. Holding each end of one tie, wrap each around towel roll and tie ends in a bow at center top, rep with rem tie on opposite end. ◆

Busy Baby CONTINUED FROM PAGE 103 ▶

2, sk next 2 sc, sl st in last sc *(buttonhole)*, turn.
Row 20: Ch 1, sc in sl st, sc in each of next 2 chs, sc in next sl st, turn. *(4 sc)*
Row 21: Ch 1, [sc in next sc, dc in next sc] twice, turn.
Rows 22–37: Rep row 2. At the end of last rep, leaving a length of yarn, fasten off.
With the WS of play pad facing,

working over edging rows, measure in 12½ inches from each side edge and sew each end of handle to row 4 of edging. With WS of play pad facing, keeping work flat, adjust center of handle at buttonhole as far as possible away from outer edge of mat. Sew 1-inch button to back of play mat in line with buttonhole of strap.
Attach second strap and button to opposite edging in same manner.

Folding Play Mat
To fold the play pad to carry or store, unbutton each strap from buttons on the underside of play pad, fold each side to center, then fold up bottom to meet the top and use the handles to carry. Before playtime, use care to secure handles to underside of play pad. ◆

Crochet for Home

Home accessories, whether specially created to dress up our own decor or grace the home of a friend or loved one, are a personal expression of decorating tastes. The cozy afghans, comfortable pillows, beautiful table toppers, colorful rugs and other stylish accents included here are sure to enhance any domestic setting with their practical use and decorative appeal.

Spring Tulips

DESIGN BY
TAMMY HILDEBRAND

Pretty pink tulips fashioned from popcorns dance in colorful rows across this luscious, creamy-white afghan that's a breeze to make with double strands of yarn and an extra-large hook.

Intermediate •••

Size
49 x 70 inches

Materials
- Red Heart Super Saver medium (worsted) weight yarn (8 oz/452 yds/225g per skein):
    29 oz #316 soft white *(MC)*
    12 oz each #631 light sage *(A)* and #374 country rose *(B)*
    2 oz #633 dark sage *(C)*
- Size P/15/10mm crochet hook or size needed to obtain gauge
- Yarn needle

Gauge
Rows 1–5 = 4 inches; 7 dc = 4 inches; 2 completed tulips = 3 inches wide and 2 inches tall

Pattern Notes
Weave in loose ends as work progresses.
Join rounds with a slip stitch unless otherwise stated.
Entire afghan is crocheted holding 2 strands of yarn together.

Special Stitches
Cluster (cl): [Yo hook, insert hook in indicated st, yo, draw up a lp, yo, draw through 2 lps on hook] twice, yo, draw through all 3 lps on hook.
Popcorn (pc): 3 dc in indicated st, draw up a lp, remove hook, insert hook from front to back in first dc of 3-dc group, pick up dropped lp and draw through st on hook.
Cross-st: Sk next st, dc in next st, working over st just made, dc in skipped st.

Afghan
Row 1: With 2 strands of MC, ch 78, dc in 4th ch from hook, dc in each rem ch across, fasten off. *(76 dc)*
Row 2: Attach A with sl st in first st, ch 3, sk next 2 sts, (cl, ch 2, cl) in next st, sk next 2 sts, [(**cl** *(see Special Stitches)*, ch 2, cl) in next st, sk next 2 sts] 23 times, dc in last st, fasten off. *(48 cls)*
Row 3: Attach B with sl st in first st, ch 1, sl st in sp before next cl, ch 1, [**pc** *(see Special Stitches)* in next ch-2 sp, ch 1, sl st in sp between next 2 cls] 23 times, pc in next ch-2 sp, ch 1, sl st in sp before next st, ch 1, sl st in last st, fasten off. *(24 pc)*
Row 4: Working over sl sts of previous row, attach MC with sl st in first st, ch 3, 2 dc in sp before next cl, [sc in top of next pc, 2 dc in sp between next 2 cls] 23 times, sc in top of next pc, 2 dc in sp before next st, dc in last st, turn. *(24 sc; 52 dc)*
Row 5: Ch 3 *(counts as first dc throughout)*, sk next st, dc in next st, working over st just made, dc in skipped st, dc in next st, [cross-st over next 2 sts, dc in next st] across, turn. *(26 dc; 25 cross-sts)*
Row 6: Ch 1, sc in first st, [ch 3, sk next 2 sts, sc in next st] across, turn. *(26 sc)*
Row 7: Ch 3, [2 dc in next ch-3 sp, dc in next st] across, turn. *(76 dc)*
Rows 8–10: Rep rows 5–7. At the end of last rep, fasten off.

CONTINUED ON PAGE 164 ▶

Mountain Forests

DESIGN BY
CHRISTINE GRAZIOSO MOODY

A deep ripple design in shades of cool forest green brings to mind a lushly wooded mountainside in this beautiful afghan that works up quickly with double-stranded yarn and a large hook.

Intermediate •••

Size
48 x 64 inches

Materials
- Red Heart Super Saver medium (worsted) weight yarn (8 oz/452 yds/226g per skein):
    11 oz #312 black *(A)*
    9 oz each #633 dark sage *(B)*, #632 medium sage *(C)*, #631 light sage *(D)*, #661 frosty green *(E)* and #329 eggnog *(F)*
- Size N/15/10mm crochet hook or size needed to obtain gauge
- Yarn needle

Gauge
With 2 strands of yarn held tog, 4 sts = 2 inches; 2 dc rows = 2½ inches

Pattern Notes
Weave in loose ends as work progresses.
Join rounds with a slip stitch unless otherwise stated.
Work with 2 strands of same color yarn held together throughout.

Special Stitch
Front post treble crochet (fptr): Yo over hook twice, insert hook from front to back to front again around the vertical post of indicated st on row before last, yo, draw up a lp, [yo, draw through 2 lps on hook] 3 times, sk st directly behind fptr on working row.

Afghan
Row 1: With A, ch 115, **dc dec** *(see Stitch Guide)* in 4th and 5th chs from hook, dc in each of next 5 chs, (2 dc, ch 1, 2 dc) in next ch, dc in each of next 5 chs, *dc dec in next 5 chs, dc in each of next 5 chs, (2 dc, ch 1, 2 dc) in next ch, dc in each of next 5 chs, rep from * across ending dc dec in last 3 chs, turn. *(106 sts; 7 ch sps)*

Row 2: Ch 3 *(beg ch-3 is not used or counted as a st)*, dc dec in next 2 sts, dc in each of next 5 sts, (2 dc, ch 1, 2 dc) in next ch sp, dc in each of next 5 sts, *dc dec in next 5 sts, dc in each of next 5 sts, (2 dc, ch 1, 2 dc) in next ch sp, dc in each of next 5 sts, rep from * across to last 3 sts, dc dec in next 3 sts, turn, fasten off.

Row 3: Attach B with sl st in first st, ch 3, dc dec in next 2 sts, *[dc in each of next 3 sts, **fptr** *(see Special Stitch)* around last st before next ch sp on row before last, dc in next st on last row, (2 dc, ch 1, 2 dc) in next ch sp, dc in next st, fptr around first st after ch sp on row before last, dc in each of next 3 sts on last row], dc dec in next 5 sts, rep from * 5 more times, rep between [ ], dc dec in next 3 sts, turn.

Rows 4–50: Rep rows 2 and 3 alternately, working in color sequence of C, D, E, F, A and B, ending with row 2 and A. ◆

Sitting Pretty

DESIGNS BY
GAYLE BUNN FOR BERNAT

Dress up a new or refurbished chair with these colorful seat and back pads that work up easily in cotton worsted yarn and feature a bold pattern of bright stripes and a cheerful flower.

Easy ••

Size
Chair Pad: Approximately 12 inches
Back Chair Pad: Approximately
   12 inches

Materials
- Bernat Handicrafter cotton medium (worsted) weight yarn (1.75 oz/80 yds/50g per ball):
  Chair Pad:
    5 (10) balls #00001 white *(MC)*
    3 (5) balls each #13712 hot green *(A)*, #13628 hot orange *(B)*, #13740 hot pink *(C)* and #13742 hot blue *(D)*
  Back Chair Pad:
    5 (10) balls #13712 hot green *(A)*
    1 (2) balls each #00001 white *(MC)*, #13628 hot orange *(B)*, #13740 hot pink *(C)* and #13742 hot blue *(D)*
- Size H/8/5mm crochet hook or size needed to obtain gauge
- Yarn needle
- Straight pins
- 12-inch square cushion form
- Fiberfill

Gauge
14 sc = 4 inches; 16 rows = 4 inches

Pattern Notes
Weave in loose ends as work progresses.

Join rounds with a slip stitch unless otherwise stated.

When changing colors, work last 2 loops on hook of last st, and then draw new color through rem 2 loops on hook.

Quantity of each color of yarn listed will make a set of 2 or 4 seat and back pads. The set of 4 is in parentheses.

Chair Pad

Front & Back
Make 2.
Row 1 (RS): With MC, ch 43, 1 dc in 4th ch from hook, dc in each rem ch across, **change color** *(see Stitch Guide)* to A, turn. *(41 dc)*
Row 2: Ch 1, sc in each st across, change to MC, turn.
Row 3: Ch 3 *(counts as first dc throughout)*, dc in each st across, change to A, turn.
Row 4: Rep row 2, change to B, turn.
Row 5: Rep row 3, change to C, turn.
Row 6: Rep row 2, change to D, turn.
Row 7: Rep row 3, change to C, turn.

Row 8: Rep row 2, change to A, turn.
Row 9: Rep row 3, change to MC, turn.
Row 10: Rep row 2, change to A, turn.
Row 11: Rep row 3, change to MC, turn.
Row 12: Rep row 2, change to C, turn.
Row 13: Rep row 3, change to B, turn.
Row 14: Rep row 2, change to D, turn.
Row 15: Rep row 3, change to B, turn.
Row 16: Rep row 2, change to MC, turn.
Row 17: Rep row 3, change to A, turn.
Rep rows 2–17 for stripe pattern until pad measures 12 inches, ending with WS row, fasten off, turn.

Edging
Rnd 1: With RS facing, attach MC with a sl st to any corner st of front, ch 1, sc evenly around outer edge, working 3 sc in each corner st, join in beg sc, fasten off.
Rep rnd 1 of edging on back piece.

Gusset
Row 1 (RS): With MC, ch 11, dc in 4th ch from hook, dc in each rem ch across, change to A, turn. *(9 dc)*
Row 2: Ch 1, sc in each st across, change to MC, turn.
Row 3: Ch 3, dc in each st across,

change to B, turn.

Row 4: Rep row 2.

Row 5: Rep row 3, change to C, turn.

Row 6: Rep row 2.

Row 7: Rep row 3, change to D, turn.

Row 8: Rep row 2.

Row 9: Rep row 3, change to A, turn. Rep rows 2–9 until from beg measures length to fit around front or back, ending with a WS row, leaving a length of yarn, fasten off. Sew last row to opposite side of foundation ch.

Edging

Rnd 1: With RS facing, attach MC with a sl st at seam, ch 1, sc evenly around, join in beg sc, fasten off. Rep rnd 1 on opposite edge of gusset.

Joining

Rnd 1: With WS facing, pin front and gusset tog, attach MC with sl st at any corner, ch 1, working through both thicknesses, 1 sc in each st around, working 3 sc in each corner st, join in beg sc.

Rnd 2: Ch 1, **reverse sc** (see illustration) in each sc around, join in beg sc, fasten off.

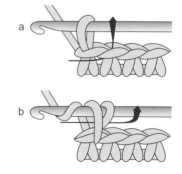

Reverse Single Crochet

Matching sts so cushion is even, pin back to rem edge of gusset, rep rnd 1 leaving 4th side open, remove hook, insert cushion form, pick up dropped lp, sc across rem 4th side. Rep rnd 2 of edging.

Tie

Make 2.

With MC, ch 50, turn ch sideways and sl st in center bump at back of 2nd ch from hook, sl st in each rem back loop across, fasten off. Fold each tie in half and sew to each back corner of cushion.

Back Chair Pad

Front

Rnd 1: With MC, ch 2, 6 sc in 2nd ch from hook, join in beg sc. *(6 sc)*

Rnd 2: Ch 1, 2 sc in each sc around, change to B, join in beg sc. *(12 sc)*

Rnd 3: Ch 1, 2 sc in first sc, sc in next sc, [2 sc in next sc, sc in next sc] around, change to MC, join in beg sc. *(18 sc)*

Rnd 4: Ch 1, 2 sc in first sc, sc in each of next 2 sc, [2 sc in next sc, sc in each of next 2 sc] around, join in beg sc, fasten off. *(24 sc)*

Flower petal

Row 5: Now working in rows, working in **front lps** *(see Stitch Guide)* of rnd 4 only, attach D with sl st in front lp, ch 1, 2 sc in same st as beg ch-1, 2 sc in each of next 3 sts, turn. *(8 sc)*

Rows 6–12: Ch 1, sc in each of next 8 sc, turn.

Row 13: Ch 1, **sc dec** *(see Stitch Guide)* in next 2 sc, sc in each of next 4 sc, sc dec in next 2 sc, turn. *(6 sc)*

Row 14: Ch 1, sc dec in next 2 sc, sc in each of next 2 sc, sc dec in next 2 sc, turn. *(4 sc)*

Row 15: Ch 1, [sc dec in next 2 sc] twice, turn. *(2 sc)*

Row 16: Ch 1, sc dec in next 2 sc, leaving a length of yarn, fasten off. *(1 sc)*

With finished petal to the right, and beg in next st of rnd 4, rep rows 5–16 until all 6 petals are completed.

Using yarn ends from each petal, sew around outer edges of petals.

Note: Now continue with front.

Rnd 5: Now working in rnds, working in rem back lps of rnd 4 of front, attach A with sl st, ch 3, dc in same st, dc in next st, [2 dc in next st, dc in next st] around, join in 3rd ch of beg ch-3. *(36 dc)*

Rnd 6: Ch 3, dc in next st, 2 dc in next st, [dc in each of next 2 sts, 2 dc in next st] around, join in 3rd ch of beg ch-3. *(48 dc)*

Rnd 7: Ch 3, dc in each of next 2 sts, 2 dc in next st, [dc in each of next 3 sts, 2 dc in next st] around, change to MC, join in 3rd ch of beg ch-3. *(60 dc)*

Rnd 8: Ch 1, sc in each st around, change to A, join in beg sc.

Rnd 9: Ch 3, dc in next st, 2 dc in next st, [dc in each of next 2 sts, 2 dc in next st] around, change to B, join in 3rd ch of beg ch-3. *(80 dc)*

Rnd 10: Rep rnd 8.

Rnd 11: Ch 3, dc in next st, [2 dc in next st, dc in each of next 4 sts] around to last 3 sts, 2 dc in next st, dc in each of next 2 sts, change to MC, join in 3rd ch of beg ch-3. *(96 dc)*

Rnd 12: Ch 1, sc in each st around, join in beg sc, fasten off.

Back

Rnds 1–4: Rep rnds 1–4 of front. *(24 sc)*

Rnd 5: Attach A in any sc of rnd 4, ch 3, dc in same st as beg ch-3, dc in next st, [2 dc in next st, dc in next st] around, join in 3rd ch of beg ch-3. *(36 dc)*

Rnds 6–12: Rep rnds 6–12 of Front. *(96 sts)*

Joining

Rnd 1: Holding front and back tog with WS tog, attach MC with sl st in any sc, working through both thicknesses, ch 1, sc in same st as beg ch-1, sc in each st around, stuffing lightly with fiberfill before closing, join in beg sc. *(96 sc)*

Rnd 2: Ch 1, **reverse sc** *(see Stitch Guide)* in each sc around, join in beg sc, fasten off.

Tie

Make 2.

Rep the same as ties for chair pad, sewing each tie to back of pad. ◆

Hanging Garden

DESIGN BY
ZENA LOW FOR BERNAT

Beginner •

Size

Fits 4–6-inch flowerpot

Materials

- Bernat Handicrafter cotton bulky (chunky) weight yarn (1¾oz/80 yds/50g per ball):
    4 balls #00083 cornflower blue *(MC)*
    1 ball each #00056 yellow *(A)*, and #00001 white *(B)*
- Size K/10½/6.5mm crochet hook or size needed to obtain gauge
- Yarn needle
- Stitch markers: 3

Display a variety of pretty flowers and plants in several of these decorative, easy-care cotton yarn hanging planters to add a lush, colorful botanical touch to any room.

Gauge

11 sc = 4 inches; 10 rows = 4 inches

Pattern Notes

Weave in loose ends as work progresses.
Join rounds with a slip stitch unless otherwise stated.

Basket

Rnd 1 (RS): With 2 strands of MC held tog, ch 5, sl st to join in beg ch to form a ring, ch 1, 10 sc in ring, join in beg sc. *(10 sc)*

Rnd 2: Ch 1, 2 sc in each st around, join in beg sc. *(20 sc)*

Rnd 3: Ch 1, 2 sc in first sc, sc in each of next 3 sc, [2 sc in next sc, sc in each of next 3 sc] 4 times, join in beg sc. *(25 sc)*

Rnd 4: Ch 1, sc in first sc, sc in each of next 4 sc, [2 sc in next sc, sc in each of next 4 sc] 4 times, join in beg sc. *(30 sc)*

Rnd 5: Ch 1, 2 sc in first sc, sc in each of next 5 sc, [2 sc in next sc, sc in each of next 5 sc] 4 times, join in beg sc. *(35 sc)*

Rnd 6: Ch 1, 2 sc in first sc, sc in each of next 6 sc, [2 sc in next sc, sc in each of next 6 sc] 4 times, join in beg sc. *(40 sc)*

Rnd 7: Ch 1, 2 sc in first sc, sc in each of next 7 sc, [2 sc in next sc, sc in each of next 7 sc] 4 times, join in beg sc. *(45 sc)*

Rnd 8: Ch 1, 2 sc in first sc, sc in each of next 8 sc, [2 sc in next sc, sc in each of next 8 sc] 4 times, join in beg sc. *(50 sc)*

Rnd 9: Ch 1, working in **back lps** *(see Stitch Guide)* only, sc in each st around, join in beg sc.

Rnd 10: Ch 1, sc in each sc around, join A with a sl st in beg sc, drop MC to WS.

Rnd 11: With A, ch 1 loosely, hdc in same st as beg ch-1, working in back lp, hdc in next st, [working in **front lp** *(see Stitch Guide)*, hdc in next st, working in back lp, hdc in next st] around, join MC with a sl st in first hdc, fasten off A.

Rnd 12: With MC, ch 1 loosely, hdc in same st as beg ch-1, working in front lp, hdc in next st, [working in back lp, hdc in next st, working in front lp, hdc in next st] around, join B with sl st in first hdc, drop MC to WS.

Rnd 13: With B, ch 1 loosely, hdc in same st as beg ch-1, working in back lp, hdc in next st, [working in front lp, hdc in next st, working in back lp, hdc in next st] around, join MC with

CONTINUED ON PAGE 164 ▶

Lotus Filet

Intermediate •••

Size
16 x 27 inches

Materials
- Crochet cotton size 20 (400 yds per ball):
  - 800 yds ecru
- Size 10/1.15mm steel crochet hook or size needed to obtain gauge

Gauge
[Dc, ch 2] 5 times = 1 inch; 6 dc rows = 1 inch

Pattern Note
Weave in loose ends as work progresses.

Create an elegant tabletop accent or add a touch of old-fashioned charm to a pretty pillow with the delicate beauty of this vintage-style floral filet runner stitched in size 20 thread.

Special Stitches
Block (bl): Dc in each of next 3 sts.
Space (sp): Ch 2, sk next 2 sts, dc in next st.
Increase block/blocks at beginning of row (inc bl/bls at beg of row): Ch 5, *(ch 3 more for each additional bl inc)*, dc in 4th ch from hook, dc in next st *(1 bl inc)*, dc in each of next 3 sts for each additional bl inc.
Increase block/blocks at end of row (inc bl/bls at end of row): Yo, draw up a lp in top of turning ch where last dc was worked, yo, draw through 1 lp on hook *(base st)*, [yo, draw through 2 lps on hook] twice *(dc)*, *yo, draw up a lp in base st, yo, draw through 1 lp on hook for next base st, [yo, draw through 2 lps on hook] twice, rep from * once for 1 bl inc, rep from * 3 times for each additional bl inc.
Decrease block/blocks at beginning of row (dec bl/bls at beg of row): Ch 1, sl st in 3 sts across for each bl dec. Always sl st into first dc of starting bl, ch 3 for first dc.
Decrease block/blocks at end of row (dec bl/bls at end of row): Leave 3 sts of each bl unworked. Always sl st into last dc of bl, turn, ch 3 for first dc of following row.

Filet Right Edge
Row 1 (WS): Ch 45, dc in 4th ch from hook, dc in each rem ch across, turn. *(14 bls)*
Row 2 (RS): Inc 2 bls at beg of row *(see Special Stitches)*, dc in each dc across, **inc 4 bls at end of row** *(see Special Stitches)*, turn. *(20 bls)*
Row 3 (WS): Inc 3 bls at beg of row, dc in each dc across, inc 2 bls at end of row, turn. *(25 bls)*
Row 4 (RS): Inc 2 bls at beg of row, dc in each of next 13 dc, [ch 2, sk next 2 sts, dc in next st] 13 times, dc in each of next 24 sts, inc 3 bls at end of row, turn. *(6 bls; 13 sps; 11 bls)*
Row 5 (WS): Inc 4 bls at beg of row, 7 **bls** *(see Special Stitches)*, 19 **sps** *(see Special Stitches)*, 4 bls, inc 1 bl at end of row, turn. *(11 bls; 19 sps; 5 bls)*
Row 6 (RS): Inc 1 bl at beg of row, 3 bls, 23 sps, 9 bls, inc 3 bls at end of row, ch 8, fasten off. *(4 bls; 23 sps; 12 bls)*

Filet Center
Row 1 (WS): Ch 78, dc in 4th ch from hook, dc in each rem ch across, turn. *(25 bls)*
Row 2 (RS): Ch 3, dc in each dc across, turn.
Row 3 (WS): Rep row 2.

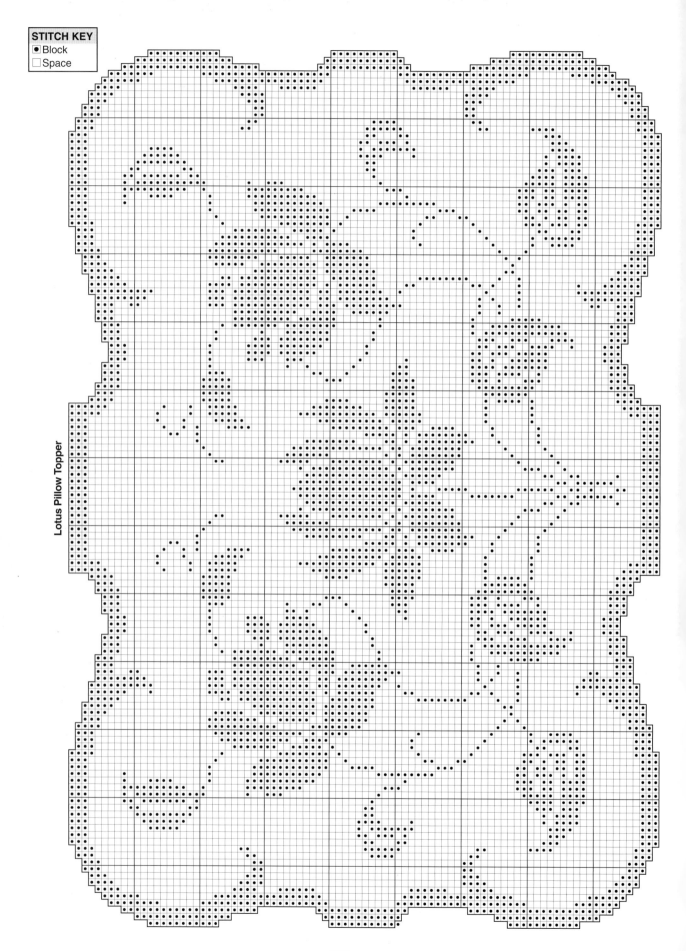

STITCH KEY
● Block
□ Space

Lotus Pillow Topper

Row 4 (RS): Inc 1 bl at beg of row, 2 bls, 21 sps, 2 bls, inc 1 bl at end of row, turn. *(3 bls; 21 sps; 3 bls)*

Row 5 (WS): Inc 2 bls at beg of row, 3 bls, 21 sps, 3 bls, inc 2 bls at end of row, turn. *(5 bls; 21 sps; 5 bls)*

Row 6 (RS): Inc 3 bls at beg of row, 4 bls, 11 sps, 1 bl, 11 sps, 4 bls, inc 3 bls at end of row, ch 8, fasten off.

Filet Left Edge

Row 1 (WS): Rep row 1 of Filet Right Edge. *(14 bls)*

Row 2 (RS): Inc 4 bls at beg of row, dc in each dc across, inc 2 bls at end of row, turn. *(20 bls)*

Row 3 (WS): Inc 2 bls at beg of row, dc in each dc across, inc 3 bls at end of row, turn. *(25 bls)*

Row 4 (RS): Inc 3 bls at beg of row, 8 bls, 113 sps, 4 bls, inc 2 bls at end of row, turn. *(11 bls; 13 sps; 6 bls)*

Row 5 (WS): Inc 1 bl at beg of row, 4 bls, 19 sps, 7 bls, inc 4 bls at end of row, turn. *(5 bls; 19 sps; 11 bls)*

Row 6 (RS): Inc 3 bls at beg of row, 9 bls, 23 sps, 3 bls, inc 1 bl at end of row, turn, do not fasten off. *(12 bls; 23 sps; 4 bls)*

Joining

Row 7 (WS): Inc 1 bl at beg of row,

3 bls, 25 sps, 11 bls, with WS of filet center facing and working across ch-8 of filet center, dc in each of next 8 chs, 6 bls, 10 sps, [1 bl, 1 sp] 3 times, 9 sps, 6 bls, with WS of filet right edge facing and working across ch-8 of filet right edge, dc in each of next 8 chs, 11 bls, 24 sps, 3 bls, turn.

Rows 8–84: Follow graph as indicated, inc and or **dec bls at beg and end of row** *(see Special Stitches)*, turn at the end of each row.

Rows 85–90: Follow graph across each section of graph, sk 8 dc sts between each section.

Block and press. ◆

Acorns & Leaves

DESIGN BY
JOSIE RABIER

Elegant crocheted lace in a repeating nature theme will add grace and charm to your fall home decor and is sure to be an eye-catching focal point wherever it is displayed.

Intermediate ●●●

Size
20 inches in diameter

Materials
- South Maid crochet cotton size 10 (350 yds per ball):
  1 ball #429 ecru
- Size 7/1.65mm steel crochet hook or size needed to obtain gauge

Gauge
Rnds 1–4 = 3 inches in diameter; 10 sts = 1 inch

Pattern Notes
Weave in loose ends as work progresses.
Join rounds with a slip stitch unless otherwise stated.

After doily is completed, ruffles are worked individually over Rnds 7 and 11.

Special Stitches
V-stitch (V-st): (Dc, ch 3, dc) in indicated st.
Beginning V-Stitch (beg V-st): Ch 6 (counts as first dc, ch 3), dc in same st as beg ch-6.
Shell: (2 dc, ch 5, 2 dc) in indicated st or sp.
Beginning shell (beg shell): (Ch 3, dc, ch 5, 2 dc) in indicated st or sp.
6-treble cluster (6-tr cl): *Yo hook twice, insert hook in indicated st, yo, draw up a lp, [yo, draw through 2 lps on hook] twice, rep from * 5 times, yo, draw through all 7 lps on hook, ch 1 to lock.
Beginning 6-treble cluster (beg 6-tr cl): Ch 3 (counts as first tr), *yo hook twice, insert hook in indicated st, yo, draw up a lp, [yo, draw through 2 lps on hook] twice, rep from * 4 times, yo, draw through all 6 lps on hook, ch 1 to lock.

Doily
Rnd 1 (RS): Ch 10, sl st to join to form a ring, ch 3 (counts as first dc throughout), 35 dc in ring, join in 3rd ch of beg ch-3. (36 dc)

Rnd 2: Ch 3, dc in each dc around, join in 3rd ch of beg ch-3.
Rnd 3: Ch 3, dc in same st as beg ch-3, 2 dc in each dc around, join in 3rd ch of beg ch-3. (72 dc)
Rnd 4: Rep rnd 2.
Rnd 5: Beg V-st (see Special Stitches) in same st, [sk next 2 dc, **V-st** (see Special Stitches) in next dc] around, join in 3rd ch of beg ch-6, sl st into ch-3 sp. (24 V-sts)
Rnd 6: Beg shell (see Special Stitches) in same sp, **shell** (see Special Stitches) in each rem ch-3 sp around, join in 3rd ch of beg ch-3, sl st into ch-5 sp. (24 shells)
Rnd 7: Ch 3, 5 dc in same ch-5 sp, 6 dc in each rem ch-5 sp around, join in 3rd ch of beg ch-3. (144 dc)
Rnd 8: Rep rnd 5. (48 V-sts)
Rnd 9: Rep rnd 6. (48 shells)
Rnd 10: Rep rnd 7. (288 dc)
Rnd 11: Beg 6-tr cl (see Special Stitches) in next 6 dc, ch 5, [**6-tr cl** (see Special Stitches) in each of next 6 dc, ch 5] around, join in top of beg cl, sl st into 3rd ch of next ch-5 lp. (48 tr cls)
Rnd 12: [Ch 7, sl st in 3rd ch of next ch-5 sp] around, join in same st as beg ch-7. (48 ch-7 lps)
Rnd 13: Ch 3, 5 dc in same st, *sl

CONTINUED ON PAGE 165 ▶

Summer Elegance

DESIGN BY
TAMMY HILDEBRAND

Bright red flowers add a splash of bold color to the lacy, join-as-you-go motifs in this light, airy cloth that's perfect for a summertime table setting. Nylon thread makes it both elegant and durable.

Intermediate •••

Size
49 x 68 inches

Materials
- J&P Coats Size 18 Coarse Count Crochet Nylon 3-ply thread (150 yds per tube):
    1350 yds #1 white
    1180 yds #38 celery
    430 yds #6 red
- Size I/9/5.5mm crochet hook or size needed to obtain gauge
- Yarn needle

Gauge
Motif = 6¼ inches square

Pattern Notes
Weave in loose ends as work progresses.
Join rounds with a slip stitch unless otherwise stated.

Special Stitches
3-double crochet cluster (3-dc cl): [Yo, insert hook in indicated st, yo, draw up a lp, yo, draw through 2 lps on hook] 3 times, yo, draw through all 4 lps on hook.

Beginning 3-double crochet cluster (beg 3-dc cl): Ch 3, [yo, insert hook in indicated st, yo, draw up a lp, yo, draw through 2 lps on hook] twice, yo, draw through all 3 lps on hook.

V-stitch (V-st): (Dc, ch 1, dc) in indicated st.

Motif
Make 70.
Rnd 1 (RS): With red, ch 4, join with sl st to form a ring, **beg 3-dc cl** *(see Special Stitches)* in ring, ch 2, [**3-dc cl** *(see Special Stitches)* in ring, ch 2] 7 times, join in top of beg 3-dc

cl, fasten off. *(8 cls; 8 ch-2 sps)*

Rnd 2: Attach celery with a sc in any ch-2 sp, (3 dc, ch 3, 3 dc) in next ch-2 sp, [sc in next ch-2 sp, (3 dc, ch 3, 3 dc) in next ch-2 sp] 3 times, join in beg sc, fasten off. *(4 sc; 24 dc)*

Rnd 3: Attach white with a sl st in any sc, ch 3 *(counts as first dc throughout)*, 2 dc in same st, sk next st, sc in next st, 5 sc in next ch-3 sp, sk next st, sc in next st, [sk next st, 3 dc in next st, sk next st, sc in next st, 5 sc in next ch-3 sp, sk next st, sc in next st] 3 times, join in 3rd ch of beg ch-3. *(28 sc; 12 dc)*

Rnd 4: Sl st in next st, ch 1, sc in same st, [sk next st, (dc, ch 1, dc) in next st] twice, (dc, ch 3, dc) in next st, (dc, ch 1, dc) in next st, sk next st, (dc, ch 1, dc) in next st, [sk next st, sc in next st, {sk next st, (dc, ch 1, dc) in next st} twice, (dc, ch 3, dc) in next st, (dc, ch 1, dc) in next st, sk next st, (dc, ch 1, dc) in next st] 3 times, join with sl st in beg sc, fasten off. *(4 sc; 40 dc)*

Rnd 5 (first motif only): Attach celery with a sl st in any ch-3 sp, ch 6, ({dc, ch 3} twice, dc) in same sp, (sc, ch 3, sc) in next ch-1 sp, sc

CONTINUED ON PAGE 166 ▶

Tempting Textures

DESIGN BY
ANNE HALLIDAY

Intermediate •••

Size
Approximately 21 x 25 inches

Materials
- Red Heart TLC Grande super-bulky (super-chunky) weight yarn (6 oz/148 yds/170g per skein): 10 oz each #2332 linen *(MC)* and #2101 white *(CC)*
- Size N/13/9mm crochet hook or size needed to obtain gauge
- Yarn needle
- Stitch marker

Gauge
2-dc cl plus 2 ch-3 sps = 4 inches

Pattern Notes
Weave in loose ends as work progresses.
When changing yarn color, leave

Soft, super-bulky yarn and dimensional stitches give this plush, cozy rug delicious texture that your bare feet will love! Stitched with a large hook, it works up super-quick!

an 8-inch length of yarn at beg and end of row to be worked into fringe.

Special Stitches
2-double crochet cluster (2-dc cl): Ch 3, [yo, insert hook in first ch of ch-3, yo, draw up a lp, yo, draw through 2 lps on hook] twice, yo, draw through all 3 lps on hook.
Bobble: Ch 4, sc in 2nd ch from hook, sc in each of next 2 chs, fold 3-sc group in half toward you from right to left, sl st in the single lp at edge of first sc made.
Join yarn with single crochet (join yarn with sc): Make a sl knot on hook, insert hook in indicated st, yo, draw up a lp, yo, draw through 2 lps on hook.
Join yarn with a slip stitch (join yarn with a sl st): Make a sl knot on hook, insert hook in indicated st, yo, draw up a lp and draw through lp on hook.
Fasten off: Ch 1, cut yarn at 8-inch length, draw up on lp on hook until yarn end draws through.

Rug
Row 1 (RS): With MC, ch 62, sc in 2nd ch from hook, [ch 3, sk next 2 chs, sc in next ch] across, fasten off, turn. *(20 ch-3 sps)*

Note: Place st marker on right side of row 1.

Row 2 (WS): Attach CC with sl st in first sc, ch 3 *(counts as first hdc, ch 1)*, sc in first ch-3 sp, work **2-dc cl** *(see Special Stitches)*, sc in next ch-3 sp, *[ch 3, sc in next ch-3 sp] twice, work 2-dc cl, sc in next ch-3 sp, rep from * across to last sc, ch 1, hdc in last sc, fasten off, turn. *(7 cls)*

Row 3 (RS): Attach MC with sc in first hdc, ch 3, working behind next 2-dc cl, dc in sc one row below 2-dc cl, ch 3, *sc in next ch-3 sp, work **bobble** *(see Special Stitches)*, sc in next ch-3 sp, ch 3, working behind next 2-dc cl, dc in sc one row below 2-dc cl, ch 3, rep from * across to last ch-3, sc in 2nd ch of last ch-3, fasten off, turn. *(6 bobbles)*

Row 4 (WS): Attach CC with sl st in first sc, ch 3 *(counts as first hdc, ch 1)*, sc in first ch-3 sp, work 2-dc cl, sc in next ch-3 sp, *ch 3, working in front of next bobble, dc in sc one row below bobble, ch 3, sc in next ch-3 sp, work 2-dc cl, sc in next ch-3 sp, rep from * across to last sc, ch 1, hdc in last sc, fasten off, turn. *(7 cls)*

Row 5 (RS): Attach MC with sc in

CONTINUED ON PAGE 167 ▶

A Patchwork Blue

DESIGN BY
RENA V. STEVENS

Rows of alternating-color stitches give the impression of multipattern blocks and the addition of surface chains complete the patchwork effect in the cleverly designed one-piece blanket.

Intermediate •••

Size
46 x 51 inches

Materials
- Red Heart Sport fine (sport) weight yarn (2½ oz/250 yds/70g per skein):
    25 oz #819 blue jewel
    12 oz #1 white
- Sizes G/6/4mm and J/10/6mm crochet hooks or size needed to obtain gauge
- Yarn needle

Gauge
Size G hook: 4 dc = 1 inch; 6 dc rows = 2½ inches

Pattern Notes
Weave in loose ends as work progresses.
Join rounds with a slip stitch unless otherwise stated.
Make color change by using new color to complete last step of last stitch made in old color, fasten off old color.

Afghan
Row 1 (RS): With size G hook and blue jewel, ch 147, dc in 5th ch from hook, dc in each of next 102 chs, [ch 2 loosely, sk next 2 chs, dc in each of next 2 chs] 10 times, turn.
Row 2: With white, ch 2 *(counts as first dc throughout)*, dc in next dc, [ch 2 loosely, sk next 2 chs, dc in each of next 2 dc] 10 times, **change color** *(see Stitch Guide)* to blue jewel, dc in each rem dc across, turn.
Row 3: Ch 2, dc in each of next 103 dc, [ch 2 loosely, sk next 2 chs, dc in each of next 2 dc] 10 times, turn.
Rows 4–20: Rep rows 2 and 3, ending last rep with row 2, do not turn.

Row 21 (WS): Attach blue jewel with a sl st in top of beg ch-2, dc in next dc, [2 dc in next ch-2 sp, dc in each of next 2 dc] 10 times, with white, dc in each of next 34 dc, [ch 2 loosely, sk next 2 dc, dc in each of next 2 dc] across to end of row, turn.
Row 22: With blue jewel, ch 2, dc in next dc, [ch 2 loosely, sk next ch-2 sp, dc in each of next 2 dc] 16 times, ch 2 loosely, sk next ch-2 sp, dc in each rem dc across, turn.
Rnd 23: Ch 2, dc in each of next 41 dc, join white in last step of last dc made, fasten off blue jewel, dc in each of next 34 dc, [ch 2 loosely, sk next ch-2 sp, dc in each of next 2 dc] across, turn.
Rows 24–35: Rep rows 22 and 23 alternately.
Row 36 (RS): With blue jewel, ch 2, dc in next dc, [2 dc in next ch-2 sp, dc in each of next 2 dc] 16 times, 2 dc in next ch-2 sp, dc in each rem dc across, turn.
Row 37: Ch 2, dc in each of next 41 dc, with white, dc in each of next 34 dc, with blue jewel, dc in each rem dc across, turn.
Row 38: Ch 2, dc in each dc

CONTINUED ON PAGE 168 ▶

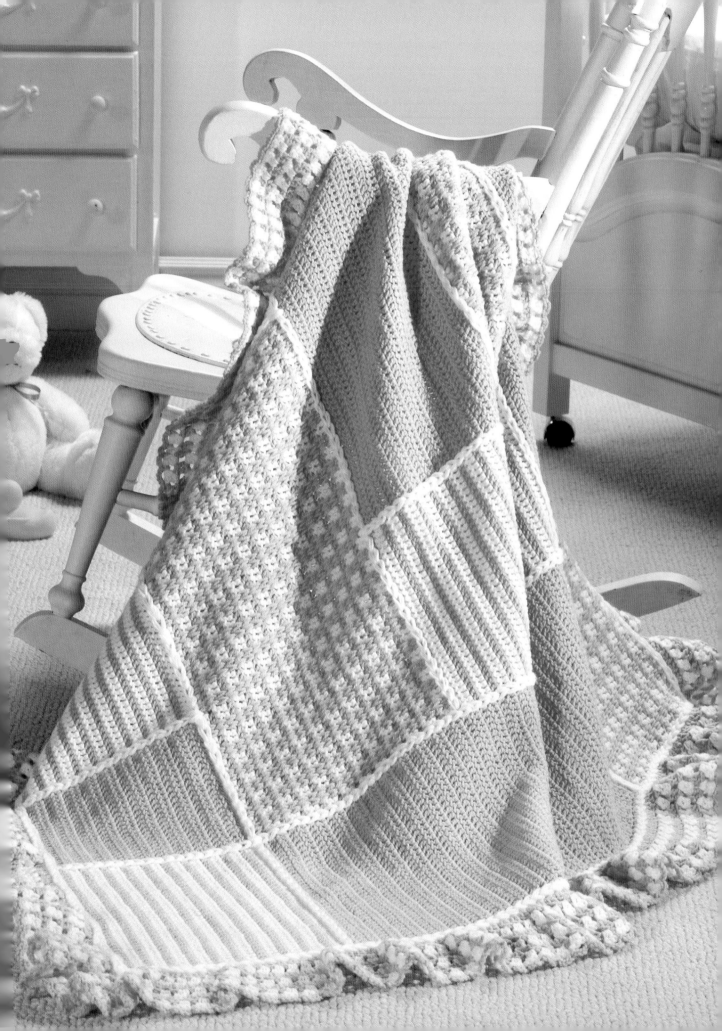

Bee Pillow

DESIGN BY
MICHELE WILCOX

The whimsical design of this cute and colorful pillow makes it hard for any child to resist! Mercerized cotton yarn makes it durable and fade-resistant for long-lasting enjoyment.

Easy ••

Size
10 inches square

Materials
- Tahki Cotton Classic medium (worsted) weight yarn (1¾ oz/108 yds per skein):
    2 skeins each #3458 hot pink and #3725 green
    1 skein #3001 white
    50 yds #3002 black
    30 yds #3532 yellow
- Size G/6/4mm crochet hook or size needed to obtain gauge
- Yarn needle
- Sewing needle
- Fiberfill
- 2 brown E beads
- Pink embroidery floss: 12 inches

Gauge
5 sc = 1 inches

Pattern Notes
Weave in loose ends as work progresses.
Join rounds with a slip stitch unless otherwise stated.

Pillow Front

Center

Row 1: With green, ch 24, sc in 2nd ch from hook, insert hook in same ch as last st, yo, draw up a lp, [insert hook in next st, yo, draw up a lp] twice, yo, draw through all 4 lps on hook (*sc dec*), *ch 1, insert hook in same st as last st, yo, draw up a lp, [insert hook in next st, yo, draw up a lp] twice, yo, draw through all 4 lps on hook (*sc dec*), rep from * across, work 1 sc in same ch as last st, turn. (*1 sc; 11 sc dec; 1 sc*)

Row 2: Ch 1, sc in first st, sc dec over same st as previous sc, in top of next sc dec, then into next ch sp, *ch 1, sc dec inserting hook in same st as last st, in top of next sc dec and then in next ch sp, rep from * across, ending with 1 sc in same st as last leg of last sc dec, turn.

Rows 3–16: Rep row 2.

Rnd 17: Now working in rnds, ch 1, work 21 sc across each edge with 3 sc in each corner, join in beg sc, fasten off. (*96 sc*)

Border

Note: Border is crocheted separately on each side of center.

Row 1: Attach hot pink in center sc of any corner, ch 1, sc in same sc as beg ch-1, sc in each of next 24 sc, turn. (*25 sc*)

Row 2: Ch 9, sc in 2nd ch from hook, work a sc dec, [ch 1, work a sc dec] across, ending with sc in same st as last st, turn. (*1 sc; 16 sc dec groups; 1 sc*)

Rows 3–8: Ch 1, sc in first st, sc dec in same st as previous sc, in top of next sc dec, then into next ch sp, *ch 1, sc dec inserting hook in same st as last st, in top of next sc dec and then in next ch sp, rep from * across, ending with 1 sc in same st as last leg of last sc dec, turn.

At the end of row 8, leaving a length of yarn, fasten off.

For next side, attach hot pink in same center sc of corner as last sc on previous border was worked on row 1 before ch 9 at beg of row 2. Rep rows 1–8 of border on 2nd side. Continue to rep border on rem two sides of center.

With rem length of cotton from each border, sew side seams.

Rnd 9: Now working in rnds,

CONTINUED ON PAGE 170 ▶

HI-FLY
HELI

The Cuddly
Beasties®
ALPHABET
Book

Ladybug, Ladybug

DESIGNS BY
**DEBRA ARCH AND
MICHELE WILCOX**

The charming and colorful ladybug is creatively brought to life in a cute-as-a-bug rug crocheted in fabric strips and a cuddly blanket stitched in cool, comfortable cotton-blend yarn.

Intermediate •••

Size

25 x 30 inches

Materials

- J. & P. Coats Speed-Cro-Sheen size 3 (sport) weight cotton (100 yds per ball):
  70 yds #0001 white
- Bright red polyester single knit fabric: 6 yds
- Black polyester single knit fabric: 2 yds
- Sizes I/9/5.5mm and P/15/10mm crochet hooks or sizes needed to obtain gauge
- Sewing needle
- Sewing thread: red, white and black
- 2 size 16mm black shank buttons
- Rotary cutter and mat

Rug

DESIGN BY
DEBRA ARCH

Gauge

Size I hook: 12 sc = 4 inches;
Size P hook: 2 sc = 1 inch; 2 sc rows = 1 inch

Pattern Notes

Weave in loose ends as work progresses.
Join rounds with a slip stitch unless otherwise stated.

Fabric Preparation

Use rotary cutter and mat to cut the fabric into 1-inch strips. Join the red strip ends with a no-sew technique as follows: cut a ¼-inch vertical slit in one end of strip. Cut a similar slit in one end of 2nd strip. Insert this end of 2nd strip about 1 inch through the slit in the first strip. Thread the opposite end of the 2nd strip back through the slit at its other end. Pull gently to snug up the ends, forming a slip knot joining. Rep with all strips to form one continuous strip.
To keep the strips from tangling, as you make this continuous strip, lower the bottom end into a large basket or clean empty popcorn tin. Keep layering the strip into the container as you make it.
Rep the same with the black fabric.

Black Center Strip

Rnd 1 (RS): With size P hook and black, ch 40, sc in 2nd ch from hook, sc in each of next 38 chs, ch 1, working on opposite side of foundation ch, sc in each of next 39 chs, ch 1, join in beg sc. *(78 sc)*

First Side of Body

Row 1 (RS): Working in **back lps** *(see Stitch Guide)* only of rnd 1 of center black strip with size P hook, attach red in first st, ch 1, sc in same st as beg ch-1, sc in each of next 38 sts, turn. *(39 sc)*
Rows 2–10: Ch 1, sc in each of next 39 sc, turn.
Row 11: Ch 1, **sc dec** *(see Stitch Guide)* in next 2 sc, sc in each rem sc across, turn. *(38 sc)*
Note: Place safety pin in base of sc dec at beg of row 11 to mark this end as the dec end.
Row 12: Ch 1, sc in each sc across to last 2 sc, sc dec in next 2 sc, turn. *(37 sc)*
Rows 13–24: Rep rows 11 and 12. At the end of last rep, fasten off. *(25 sc)*

Second Side of Body

Row 1 (RS): Working in back lps only of rnd 1 of center black strip with size P hook, attach red in first st on opposite side of body, ch 1, sc in same st, sc in each of next 38 sts, turn. *(39 sc)*

Rows 2–10: Ch 1, sc in each sc across, turn.

Row 11: Ch 1, sc in each sc across to last 2 sc, sc dec in next 2 sc, turn. *(38 sc)*

Note: *Place safety pin in base of sc dec at end of row 11 to mark this as the dec end.*

Row 12: Ch 1, sc dec in next 22 sc, sc in each rem sc across, turn. *(37 sc)*

Rows 13–24: Rep rows 11 and 12 alternately. At the end of last rep, fasten off. *(25 sc)*

Head

Row 1 (RS): Working across top straight edge of body *(opposite the end where safety pin was placed)*, with size P hook, attach black, ch 1, work 20 sc evenly sp across red body section, work 2 sc across black center stripe and 20 sc evenly sp across 2nd red body section, turn. *(42 sc)*

Row 2: Ch 1, sc dec in next 2 sc, sc in each sc across to last 2 sc, sc dec in last 2 sc, turn. *(40 sc)*

Rows 3–14: Rep row 2. At the end of last rep, fasten off. *(16 sc)*

Fabric Edging

Rnd 1: With size P hook, attach black in side edge of first sc row of head, ch 1, sc in same st, sc evenly sp across head to red body section, **change color** *(see Stitch Guide)* to red, sc evenly sp around edge of body, working 2 red sc sts across bottom edge of black center strip, sc evenly sp around edge of opposite side of body, join in beg sc, fasten off.

White Edging

With size I hook, attach 1 strand of white cotton in any sc on body,

ch 1, 2 sc in same st as beg ch-1, working around entire outer edge work 2 sc in each sc around, join in beg sc, fasten off.

Spot

Make 10.

Rnd 1 (RS): With size P hook, ch 2, 9 sc in 2nd ch from hook, join in beg sc. *(9 sc)*

Rnd 2: Ch 1, 2 sc in each sc around, join in beg sc, fasten off. *(18 sc)*

Rnd 3: With size I hook, attach white cotton in any sc, ch 1, 2 sc in same sc as beg ch-1, 2 sc in each rem sc around, join in beg sc, fasten off. *(36 sc)*

Using photo as a guide, sew spots to ladybug.

Antenna

Make 2.

With size I hook and 2 strands of white cotton held tog, ch 25, fasten off. Tie a loose overhand knot into each end of ch. Using photo as a guide, with black thread, sew knot ends to ladybug.

Eye

Make 2.

With size I hook and 1 strand white cotton, ch 2, 12 sc in 2nd ch from hook, join in beg sc, fasten off. Using photo as a guide, sew eyes centered over row 6 of head with ½-inch sp between. Sew black button centered over each eye.

Afghan

DESIGN BY
MICHELE WILCOX

Gauge

4 dc = 1 inch; 2 dc rows = 1 inch

Pattern Notes

Weave in loose ends as work progresses.

Join rounds with a slip stitch unless otherwise stated.

Intermediate •••

Size

36 inches square

Materials

- Red Heart TLC Cotton Plus medium (worsted) weight yarn (3.5 oz/186 yds/99g per skein):
    2 skeins #3001 white
    3 skeins each #3907 red and #3002 black
- Size G/6/4mm crochet hook or size needed to obtain gauge
- Yarn needle

Afghan Center

Row 1: With white, ch 51, dc in 3rd ch from hook, dc in each rem ch across, turn. *(50 dc)*

Rows 2–26: Ch 2 *(counts as first dc)*, dc in each rem dc across, turn.

Rnd 27: Now working in rnds, ch 1, work 48 sc across each side edge, work 3 sc in each center corner st, join in beg sc, fasten off.

First Edge

Row 1: Attach red in center sc of any corner with a sc, work 51 sc across *(last sc will be center sc of next corner)*, turn.

Row 2: Ch 41, dc in 3rd ch from hook, *sk 1 st, (sc, dc) in next st, rep from * across, ending with sc in last sc, turn.

Rows 3–34: Ch 1, dc in first sc, *sk next dc, (sc, dc) in next sc, rep from * across, ending with sc in turning ch, turn. At the end of last rep, fasten off.

Second Edge

Row 1: Beg in last sc before ch 41 of previous edge made, attach black with sc in same sc, work 51 sc across *(last sc will be center sc of next corner)*, turn.

Rows 2–34: Rep rows 2–34 of first edge.

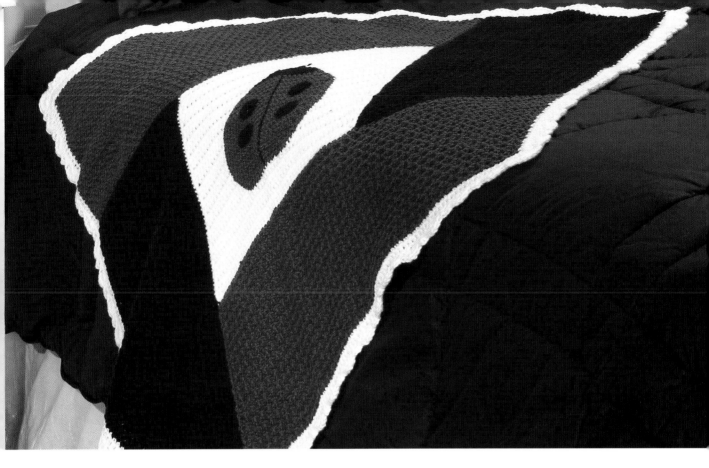

Third Edge

Rows 1–34: With red, rep second edge.

Fourth Edge

Rows 1–34: With black, rep second edge.
Using photo as a guide, with yarn needle and matching yarn, sew seams.

Edging

Rnd 1: Beg in any corner, attach white, ch 1, work 3 sc in each corner and 124 sc across each edge between corners, join in beg sc.
Rnd 2: Ch 2 *(counts as first dc throughout)*, dc in same st as beg ch-2, *3 dc in next sc, 2 dc in next sc, dc in each of next 124 sc**, 2 dc in next sc, rep from * around, ending last rep at **, join in 2nd ch of beg ch-2.
Rnd 3: Ch 1, sc in same st as joining, *7 dc in center corner dc of 3-dc group, sk next 2 dc, sc in next dc, ch 3, sc in next dc, sk next 2 dc, (7 dc in next dc, sk next 2 dc, sc in next dc, ch 3**, sc in next dc,

sk next 2 dc) across to next corner, rep from * around, ending last rep at **, join in beg sc, fasten off.

Ladybug

Row 1: Beg at bottom, with red, ch 15, sc in 2nd ch from hook, sc in each rem ch across, turn. *(14 sc)*
Row 2: Ch 1, 2 sc in first sc, sc in each sc across to last sc, 2 sc in last sc, turn. *(16 sc)*
Row 3: Rep row 2. *(18 sc)*
Row 4: Ch 1, sc in each sc across, turn.
Rows 5 & 6: Rep row 2. *(22 sc)*
Rows 7 & 8: Rep row 4.
Row 9: Rep row 2. *(24 sc)*
Row 10: Rep row 4.
Row 11: Rep row 2. *(26 sc)*
Rows 12–22: Rep row 4.
Row 23: Ch 1, sc dec in next 2 sc, sc in each sc across to last 2 sc, sc dec in next 2 sc, turn. *(24 sc)*
Row 24: Rep row 4.
Rows 25–28: Rep rows 23 and 24. *(20 sc)*
Rows 29–31: Rep row 23. At the end of last rep, fasten off. *(14 sc)*

Row 32: Attach black in first sc, ch 1, sc in each st across, turn.
Row 33: Rep row 4.
Rows 34–36: Rep row 23. At the end of last rep, fasten off. *(8 sc)*
With length of black and yarn needle, embroider **back st** *(see illustration)* up center of red body.

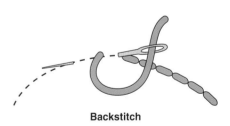

Backstitch

Spot

Make 6.

Rnd 1: With black, ch 2, 6 sc in 2nd ch from hook, join in beg sc. *(6 sc)*
Rnd 2: Ch 1, 2 sc in each sc around, join in beg sc, fasten off. *(12 sc)*
Using photo as a guide, sew spots to body.
Sew ladybug in place at center of afghan. ◆

Clowning Around

DESIGN BY
ANGEL RHETT

Intermediate •••

Size
40½ x 48½ inches

Materials
- Red Heart Classic medium (worsted) weight yarn (3½ oz/198 yds/99g per skein):
    - 18 oz #412 silver
    - 8 oz #848 skipper blue
    - 6 oz #588 amethyst
    - 4 oz #1 white
    - 3 oz #253 tangerine
    - 1 oz each #676 emerald green, #230 yellow and #12 black
    - ½ oz each #730 grenadine and #902 jockey red
    - ¼ oz each #853 soft navy, #245 orange #245 and #111 eggshell
- Size G/6/4mm crochet hook or size needed to obtain gauge
- Yarn needle

Captivating and colorful, the beloved circus clown is winningly created in this simple single crochet blanket that is sure to bring smiles to a fun-loving child.

Gauge
4 sc = 1 inch; 4 sc rows = 1 inch

Pattern Notes
Graph-reading knowledge is necessary. Right side rows of graph are read from right to left and wrong side rows are read left to right.

Weave in loose ends as work progresses.

Join rounds with a slip stitch unless otherwise stated.

Afghan
Row 1: Starting at bottom edge of afghan, with silver, ch 145, sc in 2nd ch from hook, sc in each rem ch across, turn. *(144 sc)*

Rows 2–199: Following graph, ch 1, sc in each st across, **changing colors** *(see Stitch Guide)* according to graph, turn at the end of each row. At the end of row 199, fasten off.

Border
Rnd 1 (RS): Attach white in any corner, ch 3 *(counts as first dc throughout)*, 2 dc in same corner st, dc evenly sp across to next corner, [3 dc in corner st, dc evenly sp across edge] around, join in 3rd ch of beg ch-3.

Rnd 2: Ch 3, [3 dc in center corner dc, dc in each dc across edge to next corner] around, join in 3rd ch of beg ch-3, fasten off.

Rnd 3: Attach skipper blue in center corner dc, ch 1, [(sc, ch 2, sc) in center corner dc, sc in each dc across to next center corner dc] around, join in beg sc.

Rnd 4: Sl st into corner ch-2 sp, ch 6 *(counts as first tr, ch 2)*, tr in same corner sp, sk 1 st, dc in next st, hdc in next st, ch 3, sk next 2 sts, *[hdc in next st, dc in next st, (tr, ch 2, tr) in next st, dc in next st, hdc in next st, ch 3, sk next 2 sts] across to 3 sts from corner ch-2 sp, hdc in next st, dc in next st, sk next st, (tr, ch 2, tr) in corner ch-2 sp, sk next st, dc in next st, hdc in next st, ch 3, sk next 2 sts, rep from * around, ending with join in 4th ch of beg ch-6.

Rnd 5: Sl st into corner ch sp, ch 1, (sc, ch 3, sc) in corner ch sp, sc in each of next 2 sts, sk next st, working over next ch-3 sp, sc in each of next 2 sk sc of rnd 3, *sk next hdc, sc in each of next 2 sts, (sc, ch 3, sc) in next ch-2 sp, sc in each of next 2 sts, sk next hdc, working over ch-3 sp, sc in each of next 2 sk sc of rnd 3, rep from * around, ending with sk last hdc, sc in each of next 2 sts, join in beg sc, fasten off. ◆

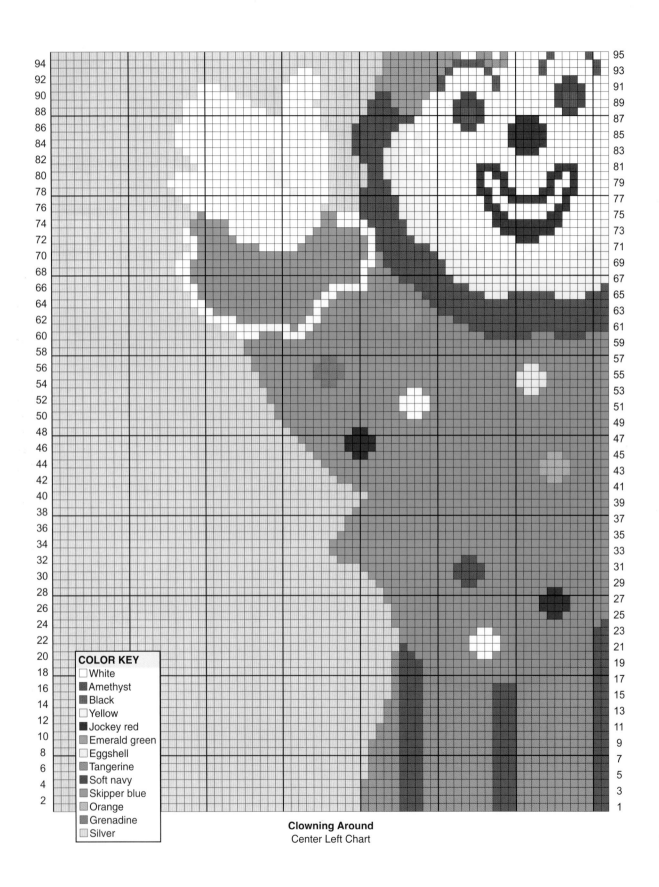

COLOR KEY
- White
- Amethyst
- Black
- Yellow
- Jockey red
- Emerald green
- Eggshell
- Tangerine
- Soft navy
- Skipper blue
- Orange
- Grenadine
- Silver

Clowning Around
Center Left Chart

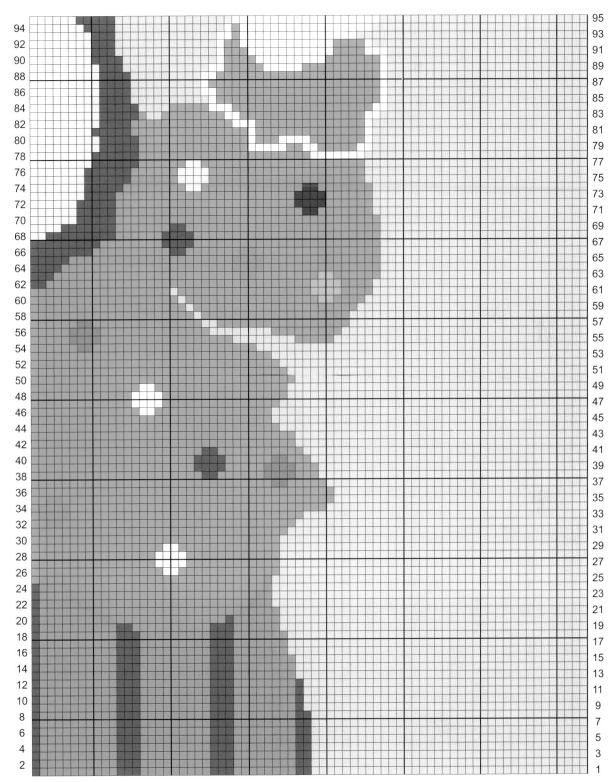

Clowning Around
Center Right Chart

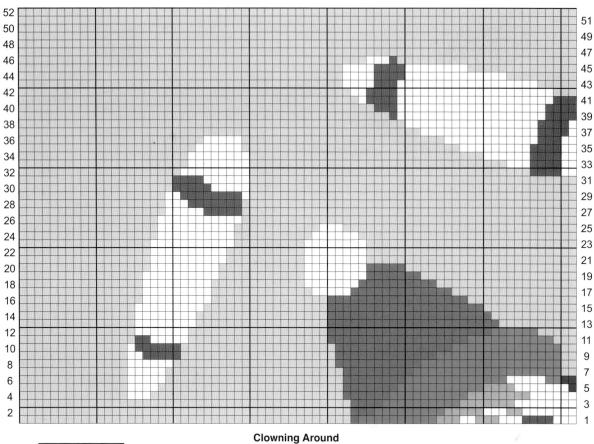

Clowning Around
Upper Left Chart

COLOR KEY
- ☐ White
- ■ Amethyst
- ■ Black
- ☐ Yellow
- ■ Jockey red
- ■ Emerald green
- ☐ Eggshell
- ■ Tangerine
- ■ Soft navy
- ■ Skipper blue
- ☐ Orange
- ■ Grenadine
- ☐ Silver

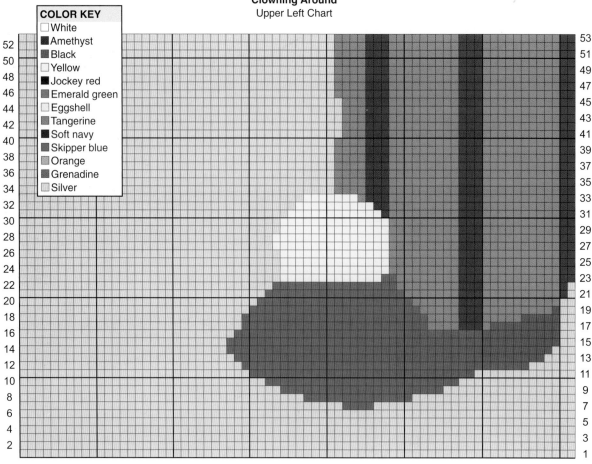

Clowning Around
Lower Left Chart

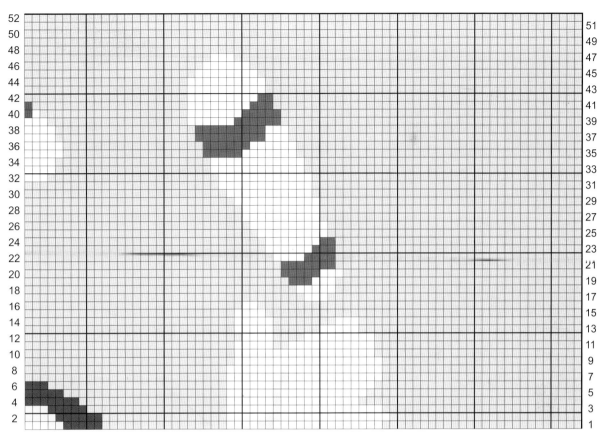

Clowning Around
Upper Right Chart

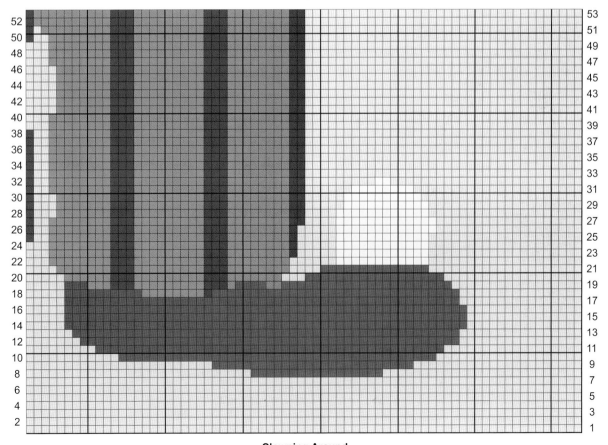

Clowning Around
Lower Right Chart

Crochet for Home

Stripes & Swirls

DESIGNS BY
DARLA SIMS

Easy ••

Size
Stripes: 14 inches square

Materials
- Lion Brand Microspun fine (sport) weight yarn (2.5 oz/168 yds/70g per skein):
    2 #194 lime
    1 each #147 purple and #148 turquoise
- Lion Brand Fun Fur bulky (chunky) eyelash yarn (1¾ oz/60 yds/50g per skein):
    2 each #194 lime and #191 violet
    1 #148 turquoise
- Size K/10½/6.5mm crochet hook or size needed to obtain gauge
- Yarn needle
- 14-inch square pillow form
- Stitch marker

Punch up your decor with a pair of trendy accent pillows worked in luscious eyelash and microfiber yarns in a fun pattern of bold, colorful stripes.

Stripes

Gauge
5 sc = 2 inches; 6 sc rnds = 2 inches

Pattern Notes
Weave in loose ends as work progresses.

Join rounds with a slip stitch unless otherwise stated.

Work with 1 strand each Fun Fur and Microspun of like colors held together throughout in the combination of, lime/lime, purple/violet and turquoise/turquoise. The fur is forced to back of work as work progresses, making the usual wrong side of the work the right side. Pillow is designed to be smaller than pillow form as fabric created from crochet tends to be elastic, thus pattern has been designed so pillow cover fits snugly and stays in place.

Pillow
Rnd 1: With lime and lime ch 31, sc in 2nd ch from hook, sc in each rem ch across, working on opposite side of foundation ch, sc in each ch across, join in beg sc, place a st marker on last st and move at the end of each rnd. *(60 sc)*

Rnd 2: Ch 1, sc in each sc around, join in beg sc.

Rnds 3–6: Rep rnd 2. At the end of last rep, fasten off.

Rnds 7–10: Attach purple and violet, rep rnd 2. At the end of last rep, fasten off.

Rnds 11–14: Attach turquoise and turquoise, rep rnd 2. At the end of last rep, fasten off.

Rnds 15–18: Rep rnds 7–10.

Rnds 19–22: Attach lime and lime, rep rnd 2. At the end of last rep, fasten off.

Rnds 23–26: Rep rnds 7–10.

Rnds 27–30: Rep rnds 11–14.

Rnds 31–34: Rep Rnds 7–10.

Rnds 35–42: Attach lime and lime, rep rnd 2. At the end of last rep, fasten off.

Turn crocheted pillow inside out so the furriest side is on outer side. Insert pillow form into crocheted pillow. Thread a length of lime sport yarn onto yarn needle and working through both lps of sts, whipstitch opening closed.

Swirls

Gauge
5 sc = 2 inches; 6 sc rnds = 2 inches

Pattern Notes
Weave in loose ends as work

CONTINUED ON PAGE 171 ▶